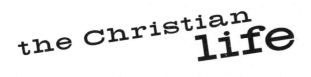

the Christian life

UNCOMMON
be extraordinary

high school edition

jim burns
general editor

the Christian
life

Published by Gospel Light
Ventura, California, U.S.A.
www.gospellight.com
Printed in the U.S.A.

Opening devotions for unit 1 and all sessions written by Joey O'Connor.
Opening introduction to unit 2 and 3 written by Jim Burns.
Study questions written by Kate Bayless.

Library of Congress Cataloging-in-Publication Data
Burns, Jim.
Uncommon high school Bible study series : the Christian life / Jim Burns.
p. cm.
ISBN 978-0-8307-4644-6 (trade paper)
1. Christian life—Biblical teaching. 2. High school students—Religious life. I. Title.
BS680.C47B88 2008
268'.433—dc22
2008019459

1 2 3 4 5 6 7 8 9 10 / 15 14 13 12 11 10 09 08

Rights for publishing this book outside the U.S.A. or in non-English languages are
administered by Gospel Light Worldwide, an international not-for-profit ministry.
For additional information, please visit www.glww.org, email info@glww.org, or write
to Gospel Light Worldwide, 1957 Eastman Avenue, Ventura, CA 93003, U.S.A.

dedication

to Jill Corey

Your partnership in our ministry is . . .
Your commitment to this cause is . . .
Your selflessness and dedication is . . .
Your longtime friendship is . . .

INCREDIBLE!

You are truly an incredible and remarkable person.
Thank you for your years of support and leadership.
You are loved and appreciated.
Love in Christ,
Jim

contents

how to use the *uncommon* group Bible studies

Each *Uncommon* Group Bible Study contains 12 sessions, which are divided into 3 stand-alone units of 4 sessions each. You may choose to teach all 12 sessions consecutively, to use just one unit, or to present individual sessions. You know your group, so do what works best for you and your students.

This is your leader's guidebook for teaching your group. Elecronic files (in PDF format) of each session's student handouts are available on *The Christian Life* DVD. The handouts include the "message," "dig," "apply," "reflect" and "meditate" sections of each study and have been formatted for easy printing. You may print as many copies as you need for your group.

Each session opens with a devotional meditation written for you, the youth leader. As hectic and trying as youth work is much of the time, it's important never to neglect your interior life. Use the devotions to refocus your heart and prepare yourself to share with kids the message that has already taken root in you. Each of the 12 sessions are divided into the following sections:

starter

Young people will stay in your youth group if they feel comfortable and make friends in the group. This section is designed for you and the students to get to know each other better. After the activity, you can show the introduction to the session from Jim Burns on *The Christian Life* DVD.

message

The message section will introduce the Scripture reading for the session and get students thinking about how the passage applies to their lives.

dig

Many young people are biblically illiterate. In this section, students will dig into the Word of God and the biblical story being presented.

apply

Young people need the opportunity to think through the issues at hand. This section will get students talking about the passage of Scripture and interacting on important issues.

reflect

The conclusion to the study will allow students to reflect on the issues presented in the Scripture reading on a more personal level.

meditate

A closing Scripture for the students to read and reflect on.

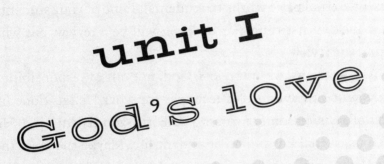

unit I
God's love

A youth pastor was once asked to speak at a large youth gathering on the East Coast. He was intimidated by the size of this huge event and by the talent of the other speakers and musicians. As he began to talk to the students about the generous gift of God's love, he apologized for giving such a simple message.

A close friend of the pastor came up to him at the conclusion of the message and said, "Great presentation. However, I have a bone to pick with you."

"Okay, let 'er rip," the pastor sheepishly responded.

"You apologized for giving a simple gospel presentation on the love of God." He went on to confront the pastor, saying, "The love of God is the simplest message of all and the deepest at the same time. Judging from the response of this crowd of kids, they needed to be reminded that God loves them unconditionally. Please don't ever apologize for the beauty of the gospel."

The pastor realized that his friend was right. His apology had been more to his communicator peers than to the kids. There is absolutely nothing more important or exciting, whether it is heard for the first time or the one-thousandth time, that "for God so loved the world that he gave his one and only Son, that whoever believes in him shall not perish but have eternal life" (John 3:16).

In this section, you have the incredible opportunity to give your students the basics of the faith. What a joy and a privilege it is to present eternal basic truths to students! Some of your students will get it for the first time. For others it will be a review, but what an important review.

As Christians, we are to love God, not out of responsibility and works, but simply out of a response for what He has done for us. After all, His reason for coming to Earth was redemption. He has given us eternal life and an abundant life. Maybe the great theologian Vince Lombardi was right when he said, "When you stray away from the basics, you've gone a long way toward defeat."

If you can place these beautiful timeless principles of basic Christianity into the lives of your students, you will have given them the most important treasure available. Let's pray that God works wonders as you faithfully share His eternal truths with them.

God's unconditional love

But God demonstrates his own love for us in this:
While we were still sinners, Christ died for us.

ROMANS 5:8

Do you remember when you used to play games as a kid and every-one would cry out, "Me first! Me first!" It didn't matter if you were playing baseball, breaking a piñata at a birthday party or running to the drinking fountain after a long, hot game of kickball. Almost everyone had a "me first" attitude.

Some things never change. The "me first" or "who's best" atti-tudes are still used by many adults to measure who has the biggest house or the nicest car or who took the most exotic vacation. It's called the "comparison game." It's a game that no one wins and everyone loses. Either I'm better than you or you're better than me, and it all depends on how much stuff we each have.

That's the me-first attitude in operation. It's a self-centered attitude that doesn't have youth ministry high on the priority list. Why?

Because giving and serving teenagers challenges the me-first attitude by honoring young people and serving their needs.

God has always had a "you first" attitude. The cornerstone of
the Christian faith is found in God's giving sacrificial and unconditional love for you. First John 4:19 says that we love God because He
first loved us. God placed you and me before Himself. Jesus Christ
gave up His life that we might have life in Him.

When was the last time you reminded yourself of the unconditional love that God has for you? Too often, youth workers focus on
telling young people about God's unconditional love but in the process forget to remind themselves of God's enduring love for them.
And not only do you need to remind yourself of that love, but you
need to experience it as well. God wants His unconditional love to
transform not only teenagers but your life as well.

God's unconditional love

starter

LOVE SONG: Divide the students into teams and have them work together to write down as many song titles as they can that contain the word "love." The team with the most legitimate names wins. Now insert *The Christian Life* DVD and watch session 1—an introduction to this study from Jim Burns.

message

God's unconditional love. It seems like such a simple concept, yet it is one of the hardest to understand. A love that is not based on who we are, where we have come from, or what we have done in our past. A love that stays constant even when we don't want it, don't deserve it, or don't even know about it. It doesn't waiver. It doesn't change. It doesn't end. Even when we are at our worst, God's love remains true.

Each one of us is sinful, broken and undeserving, and yet God gives us His love without conditions and without limits. What does it really mean to love like that? Why us? How should we respond?

Read the following verses from Luke 15:11-32. In this passage, Jesus is speaking in parables to a crowd that included people from all walks of life—from the rule-abiding Pharisees and teachers of the law to tax collectors and social outcasts. He often used parables or short stories to help His listeners better understand a key point by using situations or circumstances the audience would be familiar with.

As you read the following passage, keep these questions in mind: (1) Who might the different characters in the parable represent? (2) What point is Jesus trying to illustrate in the passage?

Jesus continued: "There was a man who had two sons. The younger one said to his father, 'Father, give me my share of the estate.' So he divided his property between them.

"Not long after that, the younger son got together all he had, set off for a distant country and there squandered his wealth in wild living. After he had spent everything, there was a severe famine in that whole country, and he began to be in need. So he went and hired himself out to a citizen of that country, who sent him to his fields to feed pigs. He longed to fill his stomach with the pods that the pigs were eating, but no one gave him anything.

"When he came to his senses, he said, 'How many of my father's hired men have food to spare, and here I am starving to death! I will set out and go back to my father and say to him: Father, I have sinned against heaven and against you. I am no longer worthy to be called your son; make me like one of your hired men.' So he got up and went to his father.

"But while he was still a long way off, his father saw him and was filled with compassion for him; he ran to his son, threw his arms around him and kissed him.

"The son said to him, 'Father, I have sinned against heaven and you. I am no longer worthy to be called your son.'

"But the father said to his servants, 'Quick! Bring the best robe and put it on him. Put a ring on his finger and sandals on his feet. Bring the fattened calf and kill it. Let's have a feast and celebrate. For this son of mine was dead and is alive again; he was lost and is found.' So they began to celebrate.

"Meanwhile, the older son was in the field. When he came near the house, he heard music and dancing. So he called one of the servants and asked him what was going on. 'Your brother has come,' he replied, 'and your father has killed the fattened calf because he has him back safe and sound.'

"The older brother became angry and refused to go in. So his father went out and pleaded with him. But he answered his father, 'Look! All these years I've been slaving for you and never disobeyed your orders. Yet you never gave me even a young goat so I could celebrate with my friends. But when this son of yours who has squandered your property with prostitutes comes home, you kill the fattened calf for him!'

" 'My son,' the father said, 'you are always with me, and everything I have is yours. But we had to celebrate and be glad, because this brother of yours was dead and is alive again; he was lost and is found' " (Luke 15:11-32).

dig

1. What might have motivated the younger brother to demand his half of the estate and then skip town?

2. What are the consequences of the younger brother's actions—
    for himself and his family?

    _____

    _____

    _____

    _____

    _____

3. Have you ever felt a desire to just pick up and leave? How
    would this decision affect your life? How would it affect the
    lives of your friends and family?

    _____

    _____

    _____

    _____

    _____

4. Try to put yourself in the father's shoes. He probably wasn't
    thrilled to be giving his son half of his estate to squander. So
    why did he give the son what he asked for? How do you see
    this as a demonstration of the father's love for his son?

    _____

    _____

    _____

    _____

5. What would have happened if the father had said no to his youngest son?

_____

_____

_____

_____

_____

6. When the younger son ran away, he went to work on a pig farm (see vv. 15-16). The Israelites, like the family in the story, followed Old Testament Law and did not eat pork (pigs are listed in the Law as an unclean animal). Knowing this, what is the significance of the younger son taking this type of job?

_____

_____

_____

_____

7. Why was the older brother upset at the party the father threw for the younger son's return? Was the older brother justified?

_____

_____

_____

_____

8. Who do the characters in the story represent?

    _____

    _____

    _____

    _____

    _____

9. This parable is the third in a series of parables that Jesus told
    that focused on the depth of God's love for us. Read Luke
    15:7,10 and 31. How does God's unconditional love for us lead
    Him to respond to the homecoming of a lost sinner?

    _____

    _____

    _____

    _____

    _____

apply

WANTED: unconditional love

1. What does unconditional love look like? Imagine you are writ-
    ing a personal ad to find a friend who loves you uncondition-
    ally. What things would you expect? What would someone have
    to put up with in your life if they loved you unconditionally?

WANTED: Friend to provide unconditional love. Must be willing
to put up with my _____and my
_____. Must not
get upset when I _____or
_____ .

You must love me even though I often _____
_____ and sometimes
_____ .

Commitment-phobes need not apply.

2. Do you have people like this in your life? Who?

_____

_____

_____

_____

_____

_____

Christ's sacrifice

Try as we may, we are human and therefore not capable of giving perfect unconditional love. But God is.

He never tires, never gives up, and never turns away. He loves us so much that He sent His Son to die in our place as a sacrifice for our sins. Romans 5:8 says, "But God demonstrates his own love for us in this: While we were still sinners, Christ died for us."

While we were *still sinners*.

God didn't wait until we were obedient and good and pleasing to Him. It was when we were at our worst that He gave us His best.

1. Imagine a close friend or family member. What would you be
    willing to do for that person? Give up your time? Give up
    your money? Sacrifice your priorities in order to benefit him
    or her? Write about someone for whom you would do any-
    thing. What makes you so willing to give up everything for
    that person? What makes him or her worth it?

    _____

    _____

    _____

    _____

    _____

2. Now think of someone you don't get along with very well.
    What would you be willing to do for *that* person? Loan them
    $5 for lunch? Let them stay in your home? Donate a kidney
    to save his or her life? Write about a time you had to do some-
    thing for someone you didn't really like. How did it make
    you feel?

    _____

    _____

    _____

    _____

    _____

why us?

It's easy to do something nice for someone who is nice to you and to be generous to those who give to you. But to show love—unconditional love—to someone who at times distrusts you, doesn't listen to you, and maybe even hates you—well, that's not so easy. But that's what God does for us.

So why does God do this for us? We mess up. We disobey. We ignore God and put Him on the back burner. Why would He love us without exception when we are so undeserving? Why?

He made us. "For you created my inmost being; you knit me together in my mother's womb" (Psalm 139:13).

We are His. "Know that the LORD is God. It is he who made us, and we are his; we are his people, the sheep of his pasture" (Psalm 100:3).

He chose to love us. "You did not choose me, but I chose you and appointed you to go and bear fruit" (John 15:16).

going it alone

1. Not only does God love you unconditionally, but He also has a design for your life. Read Jeremiah 29:11. What plans does God have for you?

    _____

    _____

    _____

    _____

    _____

Unfortunately, in spite of the unending love and guidance of the God of the Universe, many people believe that *they* can do it better and that *they* know what's best for their lives.

2. What causes people's desire to go it alone and just do things their own way?

    _____

    _____

    _____

    _____

    _____

3. In what areas of your own life have you strayed from your heavenly Father in order to do your own thing?

    _____

    _____

    _____

    _____

    _____

4. Who do you want to be in control of your life? Think about the benefits of each.

    Benefits of God in Control   Benefits of Me in Control

    _____   _____

    _____   _____

    _____   _____

    _____   _____

    _____   _____

reflect

Once you have accepted Christ into your heart, no matter what you do or don't do, God loves you! The love you receive from family or friends can change. God's love for you always remains the same because God doesn't change. While we may understand this love in our heads, it may be more difficult to truly feel. Take a moment to consider the full meaning of a God who loves you without conditions.

1. Why is it often difficult to receive unconditional love from God or even from others?

_____

_____

_____

_____

_____

2. According to the following verses, what should your response be to God's unconditional love?

John 13:34: _____

_____

1 John 4:11: _____

_____

Psalm 95:6-7: _____

_____

Psalm 66:20: _____

_____

3. How would the Christian faith be different if God's love *was* conditional and based on what you did?

_____

_____

_____

_____

4. How do you think your life would be different if you trusted God completely and let Him lead every aspect of your life?

_____

_____

_____

_____

5. Oftentimes, it is hard to understand God's plan at the moment because we cannot see the big picture. Our site is limited; God's view is infinite. Describe a time when it was only after the fact that you realized the perfect nature of God's plan.

meditation

Neither height nor depth, nor anything else in all creation,

will be able to separate us from the love of God

that is in Christ Jesus our Lord.

ROMANS 8:39

new life

> *Her papery skin a ghostly, grayish white, her gums bleeding and her*
> *heartbeat irregular, Christy Henrich withered to little more than a*
> *skeleton. She was engaged to be married and still hadn't reached*
> *puberty at 22, her emaciated body tricked her into perpetual childhood*
> *by a self-inflicted starvation diet that led her to death two weeks ago.*
>
> SAN DIEGO UNION-TRIBUNE, AUGUST 9, 1994

In a nation full of food, it's difficult to imagine a person starving herself to death. Christy Henrich, a former Olympic gymnast, died of multiple organ system failure after a decade-long, intense struggle with anorexia and bulimia. Her tragic death was the sad consequence of a ruthless eating disorder that literally devours its victims. Couldn't the same tragedy be said of the millions of people whose hearts and souls are starving for new life in Christ?

New life in Jesus Christ is the solid answer to a starving world full of hungry hearts. Though Christy Henrich refused to eat the food that provided health and life to her body, it's clear that her hunger went beyond the four basic food groups. She was starving for love. For a sense of belonging. Significance. Esteem. Attention. She was starving for everything that Jesus freely gives in His love and compassion for us. Although her family members desperately tried to help her, Christy's disease distorted and warped her perception of herself and those closest to her.

What part of your heart is starving for attention? What needs in your life are screaming out in hunger? What are you looking for to satisfy you like nothing else? Just as the students in your youth ministry have special needs, wants and desires, it's critical to examine your own needs, wants and desires.

Everything that we could possibly hope for is found in Christ Jesus. He is the only one who can truly satisfy all of our needs. Material possessions, professional status, relationships, fame or fortune can never give us the truly deep and satisfying quality of life we desire. Only Jesus Christ, through the power of the Holy Spirit, can calm our restless, hungry hearts. Our souls can rest in Him. Full. Content. Satisfied.

This week, remember the wonderful words of Jesus in John 6:35: "I am the bread of life. He who comes to me will never go hungry, and he who believes in me will never be thirsty."

new life

starter

NEW LIFE: Working in pairs, see how many of the following animals you can match with their offspring. (*Answers can be found at the end of this study.*)

_____ 1. cow	_____ a. cub
_____ 2. ape	_____ b. foal
_____ 3. bear	_____ c. eyas
_____ 4. goat	_____ d. fry
_____ 5. hawk	_____ e. gosling
_____ 6. kangaroo	_____ f. calf
_____ 7. fish	_____ g. pinky
_____ 8. horse	_____ h. kid
_____ 9. mouse	_____ i. joey
_____ 10. goose	_____ j. infant

Now watch the introduction to session 2 on *The Christian Life* DVD.

message

The passage you are about to read includes one of the most famous verses in the Bible. Many of you have probably heard it, and some of you may have even memorized it: "For God so loved the world that he gave his one and only son, that whoever believes in him shall not perish but have eternal life" (John 3:16).

Often times, when we hear something repeatedly—when we become too familiar with it—it begins to lose its significance. A song played over and over again on the radio. A lecture you've heard one too many times.

This can happen with key verses from the Bible as well. Our eyes glaze over the passage, or our lips mindlessly recite the words without remembering the incredible meaning behind the verses. This time, as you read through these verses from John 3, try to read them with fresh eyes and truly hear the amazing promise Jesus makes.

For the most part, Jesus was surrounded by the ordinary people of His day. However, in this conversation, we see Him with one of the important Jewish leaders of His time: a man named Nicodemus.

So, who was Nicodemus?

He was a Pharisee. In many ways, the Pharisees were the most important people in the whole country of Israel. There may not have been more than 6,000 Pharisees at the time of Jesus, and they all were completely dedicated to observing every minute detail of the Old Testament Law. They were also violently opposed to Jesus and His teachings.

He was a member of the Sanhedrin. The Sanhedrin was composed of 70 religious leaders and acted as the supreme court of the Jewish people.

He was rich. When Jesus died, Nicodemus brought a "mixture of myrrh and aloes, about seventy-five pounds" (John 19:39) for Jesus' body. Only a wealthy man could afford a gift like this.

As you read the following passage, keep these questions in mind: (1) What does it mean to be "born again"? (2) How do we attain eternal life?

Now there was a man of the Pharisees named Nicodemus, a member of the Jewish ruling council. He came to Jesus at night and said, "Rabbi, we know you are a teacher who has come from God. For no one could perform the miraculous signs you are doing if God were not with him."

In reply Jesus declared, "I tell you the truth, no one can see the kingdom of God unless he is born again."

"How can a man be born when he is old?" Nicodemus asked. "Surely he cannot enter a second time into his mother's womb to be born!"

Jesus answered, "I tell you the truth, no one can enter the kingdom of God unless he is born of water and the Spirit. Flesh gives birth to flesh, but the Spirit gives birth to spirit. You should not be surprised at my saying, 'You must be born again.' The wind blows wherever it pleases. You hear its sound, but you cannot tell where it comes from or where it is going. So it is with everyone born of the Spirit."

"How can this be?" Nicodemus asked.

"You are Israel's teacher," said Jesus, "and do you not understand these things? I tell you the truth, we speak of what we know, and we testify to what we have seen, but still you people do not accept our testimony. I have spoken to you of earthly things and you do not believe; how then will you believe if I speak of heavenly things? No one has ever gone into heaven except the one who came from heaven— the Son of Man. Just as Moses lifted up the snake in the desert, so the Son of Man must be lifted up, that everyone who believes in him may have eternal life.

"For God so loved the world that he gave his one and only Son, that whoever believes in him shall not perish but have eternal life. For

God did not send his Son into the world to condemn the world, but to save the world through him. Whoever believes in him is not condemned, but whoever does not believe stands condemned already because he has not believed in the name of God's one and only Son. This is the verdict: Light has come into the world, but men loved darkness instead of light because their deeds were evil. But whoever lives by the truth comes into the light, so that it may be seen plainly that what he has done has been done through God" (John 3:1-21).

dig

1. This conversation between Jesus and Nicodemus can be a bit confusing. Look back over the verses and list any questions that you may have about this discussion.

    _____

    _____

    _____

    _____

    _____

2. Based on what you know about Nicodemus, what is the significance of his coming to talk with Jesus about these things?

    _____

    _____

    _____

    _____

    _____

3. Why do you suppose Nicodemus came to Jesus at night?

_____

_____

_____

_____

_____

4. Look again at verses 1-15. In your own words, what does it
    mean to be "born again"?

_____

_____

_____

_____

_____

5. What do the following verses tell you about being born again
    and the new life that follows?

    Ephesians 4:22-24: _____

_____

_____

    2 Corinthians 5:16-17: _____

_____

_____

Colossians 3:9: _____

_____

_____

6. Remember that Nicodemus was a Pharisee who believed the way to heaven was by following all of the Old Testament laws perfectly. How do you think he felt after hearing Jesus' explanation of the way to heaven?

_____

_____

_____

_____

7. John 3:19 says, "Light has come into the world, but men loved darkness instead of light because their deeds were evil." What do you think this passage means? What is the "darkness"?

_____

_____

_____

_____

apply

1. Place a mark next to the phrase below that best describes your response to the eternal message of Jesus: "You must be born again" (John 3:7).

☐ I have experienced new birth in my life.

☐ I'm not interested in experiencing new birth at this time.

☐ It sounds interesting, but I really don't understand the concept of new birth.

☐ I'm interested in experiencing new birth.

2. Why do you need to be "born again" to get into heaven?

_____

_____

_____

_____

_____

_____

3. Being re-born means that the old self must die. Think about your views, attitudes and actions. List the differences between your old self before becoming a Christian and your new self that has been born again in Christ.

Old Self   New Self

_____   _____

_____   _____

_____   _____

_____   _____

_____   _____

_____   _____

4. Reread John 3:16-18. This has sometimes been called the gospel in a nutshell, as it uses only a few sentences to tell the essence of the salvation story. Imagine a friend asks you what this whole Jesus-dying-on-the-cross thing is all about. How would you explain these three verses in your own words?

    _____

    _____

    _____

    _____

5. Even if you've already committed your life to Jesus, there can be areas of your life that do not reflect the new life you have in Christ. What areas of your life do you still need to give over to Jesus?

    _____

    _____

    _____

    _____

6. What specifically is holding you back from giving these areas of your life over to God?

    _____

    _____

    _____

    _____

7. Read Luke 9:23-25. What do these verses reveal about the cost of following Christ?

_____

_____

_____

_____

_____

8. In 1 Corinthians 15:22,31, Paul writes, "For as in Adam all die, so in Christ all will be made alive. . . . I die every day— I mean that, brothers—just as surely as I glory over you in Christ Jesus our Lord." Why must the old self die every day?

_____

_____

_____

_____

reflect

If you have never accepted Jesus as your Lord and Savior and want to experience the fullness of life and depth of His unconditional love, pray the following prayer:

Dear Lord Jesus,
I know that I am a sinner and need Your forgiveness. I believe that
You died for my sins. I want to turn from my sins. I now invite You
to come into my heart and life. I want to trust and follow You as Lord
and Savior. In Jesus' name. Amen.

Although it may appear to be a simple prayer, it will have a life-changing impact. Be sure to share your decision with your leader so that he or she can rejoice with you and provide guidance in your new walk with the Lord.

1. Once people have accepted Jesus as their Savior, why don't their lives always reflect their new selves? Why do the old selves still pop up?

    _____

    _____

    _____

    _____

2. What holds people back from starting over with God?

    _____

    _____

    _____

    _____

3. A new life in Christ does not mean an easy life. What are some of the difficulties you will face because of following Jesus?

    _____

    _____

    _____

    _____

4. What is the status of your faith right now? How are you grow-
    ing as a Christian?

    _____

    _____

    _____

    _____

    _____

5. This passage in John ends with a discussion about living in
    the truth (see v. 21). What does "living in the truth" mean? Do
    you think you are currently living in the truth?

    _____

    _____

    _____

    _____

    _____

meditation

Therefore, if anyone is in Christ, he is a new creation;

the old has gone, the new has come!

2 CORINTHIANS 5:17

Answers to Starter: 1-f, 2-j, 3-a, 4-h, 5-c, 6-I, 7-d, 8-b, 9-g, 10-e

a lifestyle of love

Let's believe in God's love, and let's be faithful to him.
If you look at the cross, you will see his head lowered to kiss you.
You will see his arms stretched out to embrace you. You will see
his heart open to welcome you. Don't be afraid. He loves us,
and he wants us to love one another.

MOTHER TERESA

Giving Jesus to others, especially young people, is something you should never be afraid or ashamed of doing. Sharing the gift of God's unconditional love is the most priceless, beautiful gift that you could ever give someone. When you share the love of Jesus Christ, you are literally sharing the opportunity of new life. Putting God's love into action requires courage, gentleness and humility as you allow Christ to work through your life.

Mother Teresa shared her love for Jesus Christ in a bold yet simple way. She was a hero of the faith because of her humble and childlike belief in God. Did Mother Teresa win the respect of millions for being a tremendous speaker? Did she win the Nobel Peace

Prize for being young and creative? Did more than 80,000 people join her missionary order because she was a brilliant strategist? All these questions receive a resounding no! Mother Teresa won the hearts of millions of people because she had a simple devotion to the Lord as seen in her work with the poorest of the poor.

St. Francis of Assisi once said, "Go into all the nations and make disciples of all men and, if you must, use words." Our lives must come before our words. Sharing a lifestyle of love first begins with your actions and then your words. People are looking for a demonstration of the gospel. When young people see the presence of Jesus Christ in your life, then your words will begin to make sense.

God wants to use you in a simple way to make major changes in the lives of teenagers. It is your ears, hands, legs, mouth and heart that are His tools for His glory. You are an instrument of Jesus Christ, an ambassador for God and a minister of reconciliation. Because of God's continual work in your life, people will have the impression that Jesus Christ has come into the world again.

a lifestyle of love

starter

THE OUTSIDER: On a large piece of paper, work together to make a list of groups of people currently or historically who have been viewed as outcasts. For each item in your list, answer the following questions:

- Why were/are they viewed as outcasts?
- Have views of these groups changed over time?
- If so, have those views changed for the better or the worse?
- What influenced or caused the change?

Now watch the introduction to session 3 on *The Christian Life* DVD.

message

Are there people in your life whom you don't associate with? Maybe certain cliques at school that you avoid? Certain groups you try to steer clear of?

In Jesus' day, there were many groups that steered clear of each other, the most famous of which were the Jews and the Samaritans. These two groups' disgust of each other was deep-rooted and based on both religious and political differences. The religious beliefs of the Samaritans were very similar to those of the Jews, but with a handful of key differences—and it was these differences that led to each group's distrust and dislike of the other. The Jews' and Samaritans' feelings went so deep that many Jews believed they could become contaminated if they passed through Samaritan territory, and went to great lengths to travel outside of those lands.

This is why the story of Jesus and the Samarian woman told in John 4:39-42 is so shocking. Not only does Jesus travel through Samaria, but He also stops to talk to a Samaritan woman. It was almost unthinkable for a Jew to speak with a Samaritan, and definitely unheard of for a Jewish rabbi to speak to a woman—much less a *Samaritan* woman. Yet in this story, we find Jesus not only speaking to her but also asking to share a drink of water and caring for her spiritual relationship with God.

As you read the following passage, keep these questions in mind: (1) If you were the Samaritan woman and Jesus suddenly approached and began talking with you, what thoughts would be going through your mind? (2) What was the impact of Jesus' simple yet extraordinary conversation with the Samaritan woman?

Now he had to go through Samaria. So he came to a town in Samaria called Sychar, near the plot of ground Jacob had given to his son Joseph. Jacob's well was there, and Jesus, tired as he was from the journey, sat down by the well. It was about the sixth hour.

When a Samaritan woman came to draw water, Jesus said to her, "Will you give me a drink?" (His disciples had gone into the town to buy food.)

The Samaritan woman said to him, "You are a Jew and I am a Samaritan woman. How can you ask me for a drink?" (For Jews do not associate with Samaritans.)

Jesus answered her, "If you knew the gift of God and who it is that asks you for a drink, you would have asked him and he would have given you living water."

"Sir," the woman said, "you have nothing to draw with and the well is deep. Where can you get this living water? Are you greater than our father Jacob, who gave us the well and drank from it himself, as did also his sons and his flocks and herds?"

Jesus answered, "Everyone who drinks this water will be thirsty again, but whoever drinks the water I give him will never thirst. Indeed, the water I give him will become in him a spring of water welling up to eternal life."

The woman said to him, "Sir, give me this water so that I won't get thirsty and have to keep coming here to draw water."

He told her, "Go, call your husband and come back."

"I have no husband," she replied.

Jesus said to her, "You are right when you say you have no husband. The fact is, you have had five husbands, and the man you now have is not your husband. What you have just said is quite true."

"Sir," the woman said, "I can see that you are a prophet. Our fathers worshiped on this mountain, but you Jews claim that the place where we must worship is in Jerusalem."

Jesus declared, "Believe me, woman, a time is coming when you will worship the Father neither on this mountain nor in Jerusalem. You Samaritans worship what you do not know; we worship what we do know, for salvation is from the Jews. Yet a time is coming and has now come when the true worshipers will worship the Father in spirit and truth, for they are the kind of worshipers the Father seeks. God is spirit, and his worshipers must worship in spirit and in truth."

The woman said, "I know that Messiah" (called Christ) "is coming. When he comes, he will explain everything to us."

Then Jesus declared, "I who speak to you am he . . ."

Many of the Samaritans from that town believed in him because of the woman's testimony, "He told me everything I ever did." So when the Samaritans came to him, they urged him to stay with them, and he stayed two days. And because of his words many more became believers.

They said to the woman, "We no longer believe just because of what you said; now we have heard for ourselves, and we know that this man really is the Savior of the world" (John 4:4-26,39-42).

dig

1. John 4:4 states, "Now he [Jesus] had to go through Samaria." We previously mentioned how Jews frequently went out of their way to avoid going through Samaria, sometimes taking lengthy and difficult detours. Yet the text says that Jesus *had* to go through the land. Why?

2. From the text, what do you learn about the Samaritan woman?

3. John 4:6 states that the woman came to the well at the sixth hour—the hottest part of the day. Everyone else was home resting during this time. Based on what is known about her, why might the woman have chosen this time to come to the well?

_____

_____

_____

_____

_____

4. What do you think Jesus means by "living water"?

_____

_____

_____

_____

_____

5. What does the Samaritan woman think the living water is?

_____

_____

_____

_____

_____

6. What do you suppose Jesus is trying to accomplish from the conversation about the woman's husbands (see vv. 16-26)? What is the point of this conversation?

_____

_____

_____

_____

_____

7. Look again at verses 25-26. What bold—but true—statement does Jesus make here?

_____

_____

_____

_____

8. Later verses in John 4 talk about how the Samaritan woman went back to the town and told the people about her encounter with Jesus. If it had been you at the well, how would you have responded?

_____

_____

_____

_____

9. Many Samaritans from that town came to believe in Jesus.
   What two other reasons are given for why others were led to
   Jesus (see vv. 39-42)?

_____

_____

_____

_____

_____

apply

By observing how Jesus relates to this woman, we can see several important principles for sharing our faith with others.[1]

meet people on their territory

The Samaritan woman wasn't going to come out to see Jesus, so He came to see her. We can't expect people to waltz into our churches and youth groups. Think of those people in your life who don't know Jesus. In what locations could you meet those people that would still be in their comfort zone? List them here.

_____

_____

_____

_____

_____

find a common interest

Jesus immediately finds a common interest to share with the stranger: water! Despite their many differences, it is a topic to which they both can relate. Think again of those people in your life who don't know Jesus. In the space below, list their names, how you could meet them on their territory, and what a common interest might be.

Name	The Interaction	Common Interest
Example: John	*Going to a baseball game*	*Sports*

arouse curiosity about the faith

Not everyone is going to be innately interested in hearing about Jesus. In the story, Jesus engaged the woman in conversation by moving from a common interest (water) to a spiritual element (living water). Think of the names you wrote down in the question above. What are specific ways through conversation and lifestyle you could create curiosity about Jesus in these relationships?

don't be condemning

John 4:16-21 is a wonderful example of Jesus leading someone to the truth. Notice that Jesus did not condemn the woman but rather cultivated the conversation by speaking truthfully about the circumstances of her own life. He pointed out her true needs without criticizing her.

1. If Jesus had condemned the woman, what would this have done to establishing the relationship?

    _____

    _____

    _____

    _____

    _____

2. How can you let people know you care for them even when you disapprove of their lifestyles?

    _____

    _____

    _____

    _____

    _____

present the truth of Jesus Christ

Jesus confronted the woman with the fact that He was the Messiah. She had no choice but to respond.

1. Have you ever sensed God providing an opportunity for you to share the good news of Christ with someone? How did you respond?

2. If so, what was the experience like? If not, what prevented you from doing so?

3. Think about some of the names you wrote down above. What are some of your fears or concerns about sharing the gospel with these people?

4. Read through the following passages. What promises from
   God are revealed in these verses in regard to facing our fears
   about sharing the good news with others?

   Matthew 7:7-8: _____

   _____

   _____

   Luke 21:10-15: _____

   _____

   _____

   2 Corinthians 12:9-10: _____

   _____

   _____

   Philippians 4:6-7,13: _____

   _____

   _____

5. Read Mark 8:4-15, the Parable of the Sower. What is the job
   of the sower in the story? How does this relate to sharing our
   faith with others?

reflect

1. What makes it difficult for you to share your faith?

2. What happens when witnessing turns into a condemnation of non-Christians?

3. What might make people curious about Christianity? What are elements in your life that might intrigue a non-Christian?

4. Think back to the names you wrote down of people who do
    not know Jesus. Are you willing to make a commitment to
    move forward in sharing your faith with these individuals? If
    so, what is one thing in the next week you could do to begin
    the conversation?

    _____

    _____

    _____

    _____

5. If not, what is holding you back?

    _____

    _____

    _____

    _____

meditation

Always be prepared to give an answer to everyone who
asks you to give a reason for the hope that you have. But
do this with gentleness and respect, keeping a clear con-
science, so that those who speak maliciously against your
good behavior in Christ may be ashamed of their slander.

1 Peter 3:15-16

Note

1. I am grateful to Fritz Ridenour and his excellent book *Tell It Like It Is* (Ventura, CA: Regal
   Books, 1968) for first introducing me to these principles in a different form.

discipleship

We asked people if they would do any of the following for 10 million dollars. Two-thirds would agree to at least one, some to several: Abandon their entire family (25%), abandon their church (25%), become prostitutes for a week or more (23%), leave their spouses (16%), kill a stranger (7%), change their race (6%), put their children up for adoption (3%).

<small>SURVEY FROM *THE DAY AMERICA TOLD THE TRUTH*</small>

What would you be willing to do for 10 million dollars? Imagine all the wonderful things you could do with that much money. Vacations! A new Porsche! Throw in a Ferrari or two! What about that mansion you've had your eye on? Ten million dollars could go a long way! But even if you had that much money, there would still be a cost. A major cost. That's the challenge of this lesson: Are you willing to sell out or be sold out for Jesus Christ?

The goal of discipleship is to daily walk with Jesus. To do that, Jesus asks you to do two things: (1) deny yourself, and (2) take up your cross. If you are going to continue to follow Jesus, what area of your life do you need to hand over to God? What problem, sin or temptations do you need to lay at the foot of the cross today? Following Jesus is costly, because it will mean following God's will and not your own.

Taking up one's cross isn't a very popular idea. The cross is an instrument of death—a rugged piece of wood to which criminals guilty of their crimes against the state were nailed. In taking up your cross to follow Jesus, what needs to die so that you can experience new life in Christ? What struggles or hardships must you bear in the name of Christ?

The good news of the gospel is that because of Christ's death on the cross and resurrection from the dead, you don't have to bear your cross alone. Jesus is the one who gives you strength to deny yourself in order to know His love more fully. He is the one who will help you bear your cross as you follow Him.

Don't let anyone tell you that following Jesus isn't costly, but don't let anyone tell you it's not worth it.

discipleship

starter

TALKING POINTS: Around the world, more than 200 million Christians suffer persecution for their faith in Christ. Many have to meet in secret, while those who do not often risk their lives. Read the following two accounts from 2008:

> NORTH KOREA—The Voice of the Martyrs is calling on the Communist North Korean government to immediately release 10 college students in Ham Kyung Book Do Chung, North Korea, who were investigated and arrested for reading a Bible and watching a video CD about the Bible.
>
> According to Free North Korea Broadcasting, Mr. Jung, former vice-president of GumRung Company of the Rodong Dang Labor Organization Department, reported the case and has since escaped to China to avoid arrest by the National Security Agency (Bowiboo). "In March 2006, 200 Life Bibles and several hundred CDs were purchased in China

and secretly placed in flour bags before being smuggled into North Korea. This huge Bible smuggling case was headed by GumRung Company employees who were influenced by Christianity in China and underground Christians in Nasun City. All the leaders have been arrested and are being severely tortured. If I am caught, I will be sent to a prison camp for political criminals. I didn't want to die in prison camp, so I escaped," Mr. Jung said.

In the Free North Korea Broadcasting report, Mr. Jung added that most of the arrested students attended ChungJin College. "These students shared the Bible and video CD with their friends. They also distributed the Bibles and video CDs to the other college towns," he said.[1]

·   ·   ·

LAOS—Release International said today they were "deeply concerned" for the safety of at least 15 families they said had been arrested in villages in the Bokeo district. The families were from the Hmong ethnic group, who have been targeted in the past by Laotian authorities.

Release International said that in the latest raids on villages in the region several Christians had been arrested. The authorities have refused to disclose the whereabouts of 58 Christians—including women and children—seized in the latest crackdown on the church.

They added that last month the Lao authorities sentenced nine Hmong church leaders to 15 years in jail—because their Christian ministries had grown "beyond acceptable levels for the communist officials," according to news agency Compass Direct.

They say the clampdown went ahead even though their church is part of the government registered and officially recognized Lao Evangelical Church. This was part of a wider clampdown against Christians there, they suggested.

"We spoke to pastors who had been jailed simply for sharing their faith," said Release spokesman Andrew Boyd. "They described being brutally tortured and pressured to renounce their religion. When they refused they were chained with their feet in stocks in stinking cells without any sanitation. Yet many shared their faith with the other prisoners and led them to Christ."[2]

Now consider the following questions:

- How would things be different in your life if you knew you might be persecuted for your faith in Jesus?
- How would your youth group change? Your church?
- What things in your Christian life would you no longer be able to do?

Now watch the introduction to session 4 on *The Christian Life* DVD.

message

The following short Scripture reading comes from Mark 8:34-37, in which Jesus is teaching in the small villages outside of Caesarea Philippi. As you read Jesus' words, keep the following questions in mind: (1) What has it cost you to follow Jesus? (2) What would you give your life for? A person? A cause?

Then he called the crowd to him along with his disciples and said: "If anyone would come after me, he must deny himself and take up his cross and follow me. For whoever wants to save his life will lose it, but whoever loses his life for me and for the gospel will save it. What good is it for a man to gain the whole world, yet forfeit his soul? Or what can a man give in exchange for his soul?" (Mark 8:34-37).

dig

1. What does the phrase "come after me" mean to you?

   _____

   _____

   _____

2. Jesus says that we must "take up our cross." What do you think He means?

   _____

   _____

   _____

3. Summarize the following verses in your own words: "For whoever wants to save his life will lose it, but whoever loses his life for me and for the gospel will save it. What good is it for a man to gain the whole world, yet forfeit his soul?"

   _____

   _____

   _____

   _____

4. Notice who Jesus is speaking to in this passage—not just His disciples, but also a growing crowd of people who had come to hear Him speak. Imagine you are a member of this crowd and you hear this speech. How would it have made you feel? Would it have made you want to follow Jesus, or would it have given you second thoughts about being one of His followers?

_____

_____

_____

_____

_____

5. Why do you think Jesus gave this speech? What was the purpose? (For help, read the account of this story in Luke 14:27-33.)

_____

_____

_____

_____

6. In Luke 9:23, Jesus has a similar conversation with His disciple Peter. What additional information does this conversation give about how frequently we must "take up our cross"?

_____

_____

_____

_____

apply

In this passage, Jesus provides two clear requirements for those who want to follow Him: (1) They must deny themselves, and (2) they must take up their cross.

deny yourself

1. What does it mean to deny yourself?

   _____

   _____

   _____

   _____

   _____

2. You belong to Christ, not to yourself. You were bought at a high price by Jesus' death on the cross. In order to follow Christ, there is a sense of denial of your own needs for the sake of Christ's purposes. What needs, wants or desires in your life are the hardest to give up for Jesus?

   _____

   _____

   _____

   _____

   _____

   _____

3. According to Luke 14:33, how far do you have to deny your
    own desires in order to follow Jesus?

    _____

    _____

    _____

    _____

    _____

take up your cross

1. What is *your* cross?

    _____

    _____

    _____

    _____

    _____

2. In the passage from Luke 9 that you read above, Jesus says
    that we must take up our cross *daily*. Why is this not a one-
    time deal? Why must you do this every day?

    _____

    _____

    _____

    _____

    _____

3. What has being a Christian cost you? What has been the cost of becoming Christ's follower in your relationships at home, at school or at work?

_____

_____

_____

_____

_____

reflect

1. What makes discipleship costly?

_____

_____

_____

_____

2. Why is it so difficult to deny yourself, take up your cross and follow Jesus?

_____

_____

_____

_____

_____

3. What would you give your life for?

_____

_____

_____

_____

_____

4. In the passage we read in Mark 8:34-37, Jesus is asking for our lives. Do you think His request is literal or metaphoric?

_____

_____

_____

_____

_____

5. Give illustrations of people you know who have gained all the world has to offer but do not have the blessings of a relationship with God.

_____

_____

_____

_____

meditation

Here is a trustworthy saying: If we died with him,
we will also live with him; if we endure, we will
also reign with him. If we disown him, he will also
disown us; if we are faithless, he will remain faithful,
for he cannot disown himself.

2 TIMOTHY 2:11-13

Notes

1. Todd Nettleton, "North Korean Students Arrested for Reading the Bible and Watching Bible Video CD," *Voice of the Martyrs*, March 27, 2008. http://www.persecution.com/news/index.cfm?action=fullstory&newsID=599 (accessed April 2008).
2. Nick Mackenzie, "Fears over Laos Christians," *Religious Intelligence*, March 14, 2008. http://www.religiousintelligence.co.uk/news/?NewsID=1754 (accessed April 2008).

unit II

setting a strong foundation

Many years ago, my (Jim's) daughter Heidi Michelle was born with a major heart complication. It was really, really hard. Yet in the midst of all of our pain, worry and exhaustion, Cathy and I were overwhelmed with the love and support of our church and the youth ministry community.

To say it was eventful is an understatement. People gave us an incredible amount of love and support. However, the best piece of advice came to me over lunch with a friend of mine a few months after Heidi's birth. Toby worked as a real estate developer, but actually he's a philosopher. He shook my hand, looked me square in the face and said, "Burnsie, nobody said it would be easy."

His greeting has stayed with me for the last six years. He's right, you know. God never promised to remove the burdens or take away the pain of living. He did promise to walk with us through the problems.

The theme of this section is the incredible words of Jesus at the end of His Sermon on the Mount:

Therefore everyone who hears these words of mine and puts them into practice is like a wise man who built his house on the rock. The rain came down, the streams rose, and the winds blew and beat against that house; yet it did not fall, because it had its foundation on the rock. But everyone who hears these words of mine and does not put them into practice is like a foolish man who built his house on sand. The rain came down, the streams rose, and the winds blew and beat against that house, and it fell with a great crash (Matthew 7:24-27).

The eternal truth of these words of Jesus is that rain, wind and storms will come to everyone's life, but the person who builds his or her life on the Rock will make it. The ones who don't will crash. I like what Gail McDonald once said: "Untended fires soon become nothing but a pile of ashes." Part of any good youth program is not just telling your students about Jesus but also tending to the spiritual fires of your students. You need to help these young Christians build up a solid enough faith so that they can stand when the storms of life come—and the storms *will* come.

You may be like me and not be able to build even the simplest of houses. But you can build spiritual truths into the lives of your students, which is the most important factor of all. I doubt if your kids will remember the setting of your group, and I know they won't remember this curriculum. Yet you have the awesome opportunity and privilege to plant the Word of God in their lives. When others are trying to tear down your students, you're helping to set their foundations.

As you go about that task, remember this great promise from God: "All men are like grass, and all their glory is like the flowers of the field; the grass withers and the flowers fall, but the word of the Lord stands forever" (1 Peter 1:24-25).

setting a strong foundation

There is so much frustration in the world because we have relied on gods rather than God. We have genuflected before the god of science only to find that it has given us the atomic bomb, producing fears and anxieties that science can never mitigate. We have bowed before the god of money only to learn that there are such things as love and friendship that money cannot buy. . . . These transitory gods are not able to save or bring happiness to the human heart. Only God is able. It is faith in Him that we must rediscover.

MARTIN LUTHER KING, JR.

Setting a strong foundation begins with asking Christ to be the cornerstone of our lives. It also means asking Him to remove all the "gods" in our lives. Martin Luther King, Jr.'s words remind us that, at times, even Christians have bowed, genuflected and worshiped things other than the one true God. Christ wants to be the cornerstone of our lives, but He leaves the decision up to us.

Setting a foundation is often a long, slow process filled with delays and setbacks. It can take longer and cost more than we first anticipated. The same is true for our spiritual lives. At times, it can seem like we're stagnant and lifeless. We see no fruit of God in our lives. We grow tired, bored and frustrated of the process that God started in our lives long ago.

Have you ever wondered when God is going to finish the work He started in your life? Read Philippians 1:6. God is faithful. And as you make Christ the cornerstone of your life, God promises to create a strong foundation. He promises to finish what He started. Yes, the process takes a long time, but God wants this process to last your lifetime so that you can experience all He is. When you put the words of Jesus into practice, there's no storm, no problem, no obstacle that you can't overcome in Christ.

Jesus didn't come to take away our problems but to give us hope and strength in the midst of them. The "gods" of our generation cannot save us from storms or bring us the happiness we desire. Only God is able. By rediscovering God, we will brush away the sand that covers our firm foundation in Christ.

setting a strong foundation

starter

MASTER BUILDER: Gather one or two decks of cards. Have teams attempt to build the strongest and tallest tower they can on an unstable surface (on a pillow, on a balled-up blanket, on grass or on rocks). Now watch the introduction to session 5 on *The Christian Life* DVD.

message

Foundations, though often unseen, are vitally important to the structures they support. Consider the following facts:

- Roots make up more than half of a tree's size and provide support and nutrients to the remainder of the tree. Without roots, a tree would die.

- Ninety percent of an iceberg's mass is hidden underwater—hence the term "the tip of the iceberg" implies that only a small portion of the whole is seen.

- The foundation of a building holds the most weight of any element in the structure. Without a sturdy foundation, a building would not function or be safe for use.

The Christian life is not easy. Following God does not give us a get-out-of-problems-free card. In 2 Timothy 3:12, Paul says:

In fact, everyone who wants to live a godly life in Christ Jesus will be persecuted, while evil men and impostors will go from bad to worse, deceiving and being deceived.

All Christians will endure some sort of persecution, struggles and trials at some point in their lives. Each of us must therefore prepare for these difficulties by developing a solid foundation to our faith.

As you read the following passage, keep these questions in mind: (1) How can you develop a strong foundation in Christ? (2) What are the consequences of not having a strong foundation?

Therefore everyone who hears these words of mine and puts them into practice is like a wise man who built his house on the rock. The rain came down, and the streams rose, and the winds blew and beat against that house; yet it did not fall, because it had its foundation on the rock. But everyone who hears these words of mine and does not put them into practice is like a foolish man who built his house on sand. The rain came down, the streams rose, and the winds blew and beat against that house, and it fell with a great crash (Matthew 7:24-27).

dig

1. How are we like the man who built his house on the rock?

_____

_____

_____

_____

_____

2. Notice in this parable that the streams rose and the winds blew and beat against each house regardless of its foundation. What does this tell us about the Christian life?

_____

_____

_____

_____

3. What do the following elements symbolize in this story?

House: _____

_____

_____

Rock: _____

_____

_____

Sand: _____

_____

_____

Rain/Wind: _____

_____

_____

4. How would you describe the foundation of your faith in Jesus?

_____

_____

_____

_____

_____

5. In your life, what are the rains and winds that test your foundation in Christ?

_____

_____

_____

_____

_____

6. Although you should prepare for these tests to your faith, according to James, you should also rejoice in these hardships. Read James 1:2-4. Why should you rejoice during times of trials and suffering?

_____

_____

_____

_____

_____

7. Read the following statement: "It is not possible to remain static in your relationship with Jesus. Either your actions and attitudes are moving you forward in your faith or backward." Do you agree or disagree with this statement? In which direction are *you* moving?

_____

_____

_____

_____

_____

apply

Building a strong foundation for our faith is vital, but it isn't easy. Fortunately, we don't have to go it alone. God is there to help. As we look through Scripture, we can see a number of guidelines for how to develop a strong foundation in Jesus.

we need a cornerstone

A cornerstone is a stone set at the bottom of a structure as a starting place. Without a cornerstone, you can't have a strong foundation.

1. Read Ephesians 2:19-22. Who is the cornerstone?

    _____

    _____

    _____

2. According to the passage, what are all these "stones" building?

    _____

    _____

    _____

    _____

God provides instruction and guidance

Luckily, God doesn't leave us high and dry. Throughout the Bible, He provides guidance and advice on how we can develop a strong foundation. All we have to do is obey His instructions.

1. Read John 14:15,21. What do these verses tell us to do if we love God?

    _____

    _____

    _____

    _____

    _____

2. What is the result of our obedience?

_____

_____

_____

_____

_____

we must set our foundation over time

A strong foundation doesn't happen overnight. In fact, setting a strong foundation is a lifelong process.

1. Read Hebrews 10:23,36. What is the reward for being persistent and building a strong foundation?

_____

_____

_____

_____

2. According to Romans 5:3-5, although it is not always pleasant, what can strengthen our foundation? How?

_____

_____

_____

_____

build on the foundation daily

Our foundation on the Lord must be nurtured and reinforced through spiritual growth.

1. Read Joshua 1:8 and Psalm 1:2-3. What is the result of spending time with God each day?

    _____

    _____

    _____

    _____

2. What are the benefits for us? For God?

    _____

    _____

    _____

    _____

3. Many people argue that they are too busy to set aside time to spend with Jesus each day. In light of this, calculate the amount of time that you spend on the following activities during an average day.

    Sleeping: _____   Watching TV: _____

    Eating: _____   Playing video games: _____

    Working: _____   Talking on the phone: _____

    Playing sports: _____ Browsing the Internet: _____

    Doing homework: _____

4. When do you set aside time with Jesus during your day? Or, if you don't already, where could you make time in the day to spend in prayer and study?

_____

_____

_____

_____

_____

As one author stated, "Don't say you don't have enough time. You have exactly the same number of hours per day that were given to Helen Keller, Pasteur, Michelangelo, Mother Teresa, Leonardo da Vinci, Thomas Jefferson, and Albert Einstein."[1] Morning or night, 5 minutes or 50, God wants to spend time with you. In the same way an athlete spends time training for an event or a musician spends hours rehearsing for a performance, your faith requires time and commitment in order to develop and grow.

reflect

1. After reading this study, how would you describe the foundation of your Christian faith?

_____

_____

_____

_____

_____

2. Discuss a time in your life when your faith was tested. What was the outcome?

_____

_____

_____

_____

_____

_____

3. Foundations need upkeep. What are you doing to strengthen your foundation in Jesus?

_____

_____

_____

_____

_____

4. What are the things in your life that attempt to crack or crumble your foundation?

_____

_____

_____

_____

_____

5. Who or what can you think of that will help you strengthen
    the foundation of your faith?

_____

_____

_____

_____

_____

meditation

Consider it pure joy, my brothers, whenever you
face trials of many kinds, because you know that the
testing of your faith develops perseverance.
Perseverance must finish its work so that you may
be mature and complete, not lacking anything.

JAMES 1:2-4

Note

1. H. Jackson Brown, *Life's Little Instruction Book* (Nashville, TN: Rutledge Hill, 1991).

session 6

obedience

*If for one whole day, quietly and determinedly, we were to
give ourselves up to the ownership of Jesus and to obeying
His orders, we should be amazed at its close to realize
all He had packed into that one day.*

OSWALD CHAMBERS

Read the headlines. Catch the latest news. Flip on any talk show.
Hear about the hottest scandal, the environment, health care, abortion, immigration, homelessness, racism, financial misconduct, politics, war and disease. Television, radio, newspapers and magazines
bombard us daily with every issue under the sun. We are "issued out"
with every single cause and controversy imaginable. In the midst of
this barrage of issues, Jesus Christ asks of us only one thing: "Will
you obey Me today?"

Obedience. That's all Jesus Christ asks of us. All the noise of the
day's issues distracts us from the call of Christ to listen and obey
Him. In John 10:27, Jesus says, "My sheep listen to my voice; I know
them, and they follow me." Following Jesus means listening to the

Shepherd's voice—the voice of the One who knows you and wants you to follow Him. Listening to Jesus' voice is the first step to following Him and enjoying a rich, abundant life with God.

What is distracting you from hearing the voice of God today? What has lured your attention away from obeying Christ? How can you focus your attention only on Christ in order to hear His voice and follow Him? What areas of your life are preventing you from hearing Jesus' voice? How will listening to Jesus bring you the peace you desire?

Obedience to Christ means freedom and obedience. God's Word is not burdensome, and His commands are never too difficult to carry out. God wants to show you what remarkable things can happen when you are totally yielded to His commands. It is for your freedom that Christ died, and it is in dying for Christ that you are truly free.

obedience

starter

TALKING POINTS: Discuss the following quotations. What does each mean to you? Do you agree or disagree with the statement? How do you define "obedience"?

- "True obedience is true freedom." —Henry Ward Beecher

- "The purpose of problems is to push you toward obedience to God's laws, which are exact and cannot be changed. We have the free will to obey them or disobey them. Obedience will bring harmony, disobedience will bring you more problems." —Peace Pilgrim

- "War means blind obedience, unthinking stupidity, brutish callousness, wanton destruction, and irresponsible murder." —Alexander Berkman

- "I know the power obedience has of making things easy which seem impossible." —Saint Teresa

➤ "Wicked men obey from fear; good men, from love."
—Aristotle

Now watch the introduction to session 6 on *The Christian Life* DVD.

message

What is obedience? What is its importance in our walk with Jesus? Perhaps Andrew Murray, a pastor and writer in the late 1800s, put it best: "The starting point and the goal of our Christian life is obedience." If there is a secret to living the Christian life, it is to be found through obedience.

The following passage contains references to many Old Testament stories with which you may not be familiar. However, note the one thing that they all hold in common: God asks individuals to act and they obey. As you read, keep the following questions in mind: (1) In what types of actions are people being obedient? (2) In what areas of your life do you find it most difficult to obey God's calling?

Now faith is being sure of what we hope for and certain of what we do not see. This is what the ancients were commended for.

By faith we understand that the universe was formed at God's command, so that what is seen was not made out of what was visible. By faith Abel offered God a better sacrifice than Cain did. By faith he was commended as a righteous man, when God spoke well of his offerings. And by faith he still speaks, even though he is dead.

By faith Enoch was taken from this life, so that he did not experience death; he could not be found, because God had taken him away. For before he was taken, he was commended as one who pleased God. And without faith it is impossible to please God, because anyone who comes to him must believe that he exists and that he rewards those who earnestly seek him.

By faith Noah, when warned about things not yet seen, in holy fear built an ark to save his family. By his faith he condemned the world and became heir of the righteousness that comes by faith.

By faith Abraham, when called to go to a place he would later receive as his inheritance, obeyed and went, even though he did not know where he was going. By faith he made his home in the promised land like a stranger in a foreign country; he lived in tents, as did Isaac and Jacob, who were heirs with him of the same promise. For he was looking forward to the city with foundations, whose architect and builder is God.

By faith Abraham, even though he was past age—and Sarah herself was barren—was enabled to become a father because he considered him faithful who had made the promise. And so from this one man, and he as good as dead, came descendants as numerous as the stars in the sky and as countless as the sand on the seashore.

All these people were still living by faith when they died. They did not receive the things promised; they only saw them and welcomed them from a distance. And they admitted that they were aliens and strangers on earth. People who say such things show that they are looking for a country of their own. If they had been thinking of the country they had left, they would have had opportunity to return. Instead, they were longing for a better country—a heavenly one. Therefore God is not ashamed to be called their God, for he has prepared a city for them.

By faith Abraham, when God tested him, offered Isaac as a sacrifice. He who had received the promises was about to sacrifice his one and only son, even though God had said to him, "It is through Isaac that your offspring will be reckoned." Abraham reasoned that God could raise the dead, and figuratively speaking, he did receive Isaac back from death (Hebrews 11:1-19).

dig

1. How did the writer of Hebrews define "faith"?

_____

_____

_____

_____

_____

2. What is the connection between faith and obedience?

_____

_____

_____

_____

_____

3. In what ways are the individuals in this passage called upon
   to be obedient?

_____

_____

_____

_____

_____

4. Hebrews 11:7 discusses Noah's obedience. Read the original
    account in Genesis 6:11-22. What do you notice about God's
    request and Noah's response?

    _____

    _____

    _____

    _____

    _____

5. The list of individuals mentioned in these verses includes some
    great biblical heroes and some tarnished, imperfect characters.
    But at some point each of them displayed obedience in faith
    to God. What does this list of the faithful tell us about the
    kind of person God is looking for in His kingdom?

    _____

    _____

    _____

    _____

    _____

apply

Doing what God asks is easy when it's something we enjoy or want
to do. It's when the request is difficult, confusing or unpleasant
that our obedience it truly tested. Let's take a look at the practices
and promises of obedience.

Jesus, our example of obedience

1. Read Philippians 2:5-11. According to this passage, what attitude did Jesus have regarding obedience?

_____

_____

_____

_____

_____

2. What was the result of Jesus' obedience?

_____

_____

_____

_____

_____

obedience involves action

1. Read James 1:22-25. In your own words, explain the analogy James uses in this verse.

_____

_____

_____

_____

_____

2. According to these verses, what is the result of obedience?

_____

_____

_____

_____

Obedience is a choice we make that demonstrates our commitment to Jesus. That's why there can't be passive obedience. Obedience necessitates an active response on our part.

God asks for obedience in all areas of our life

1. Read 1 Kings 8:61. Write and discuss what obedience to God means in the following areas of your life:

Friendships _____

_____

Boyfriend/Girlfriend _____

_____

Parents _____

_____

Parties _____

_____

Sexuality _____

_____

Worship _____

_____

Grades _____

_____

Servanthood _____

_____

2. Take a few moments to list areas of your life in which God is calling you to be obedient.

_____

_____

_____

_____

3. How will you show obedience to God in these areas?

_____

_____

_____

_____

freedom and fulfillment come through obedience

1. Read John 14:21. If you say you love God, what will be the result according to this verse?

_____

_____

_____

_____

2. Why is this such an important principle in your Christian life?

_____

_____

_____

_____

_____

reflect

1. How do the standards of society influence your obedience to God?

_____

_____

_____

_____

_____

2. God loves you! He wants the best for you! How do you think He feels when you walk away from Him in disobedience?

_____

_____

_____

_____

3. John Calvin wrote, "True knowledge of God is born out of obedience." In your own words, what does this statement mean? Do you agree or disagree?

_____

_____

_____

_____

_____

4. Can you truly know God and not obey Him? Can you obey God if you don't truly know Him?

_____

_____

_____

_____

_____

5. What can you and others in your group do to help each other live more obedient Christian lifestyles?

_____

_____

_____

_____

_____

6. Describe a time in your life when you sensed God's calling and obeyed.

_____

_____

_____

_____

_____

_____

_____

_____

meditation

This is love for God: to obey his commands.

And his commands are not burdensome,

for everyone born of God overcomes the world.

1 JOHN 5:3-4

stepping out in faith

*"I don't understand why things can't go back to normal
at the end of the half-hour, like The Brady Bunch,"
one of the kids remarks as a new mini-crisis takes its
place beside the last one nobody quite solved.
"Because," someone replies, "Mr. Brady died of AIDS."*

TIME REVIEW OF THE FILM *REALITY BITES*

For some strange reason, television has developed a false sense of reality by helping millions of Americans to believe that at the end of a 30-minute show, everything in life will work out fine. Too many people have put their faith in a false hope of a TV reality that doesn't exist. Reality has a harsh way of challenging the things in which we place our faith.

God's Word says that placing your faith in Jesus Christ will develop a firm foundation for your life. Yet how many people or things in society promise a firmer foundation than that of Christ?

A strong faith in Christ grounds you in the reality of God's love. Faith in God offers you peace and hope in the middle of your personal storms. Faith in God is a free gift designed to help you become all that God desires you to be.

Because "faith" is an intangible sort of word that can confuse young people, this lesson is filled with tangible examples of people who put their faith and trust in God. Anticipate questions from young people who want to know how your faith in Christ makes a difference in your life.

Unlike *The Brady Bunch*, God never promises that we'll have problem-free lives when we put our faith in Christ. God promises that faith in Christ will help us to experience the reality of His love and presence in our lives.

stepping out in faith

starter

TRUST WALK: Have the group divide up into teams of two, with one person blindfolded. Have the other partner lead his or her pair through a mini-obstacle course or maze. Then switch the blindfold to the other partner for the return trip. The winning team is the one who makes it back the fastest. Now watch the introduction to session 7 on *The Christian Life* DVD.

message

There is a popular saying that states, "Faith isn't faith until it's all you're holding on to." The Christian walk often requires that we step out in faith, trusting that God will provide for us. It isn't easy, but if we cling to the promises He has made throughout the Bible, we can gain comfort from the examples of His faithfulness that we read about.

The passage you are about to read out of the book of Matthew takes place after Jesus has spent a long day teaching and healing. In the verses prior to this story, Jesus has just performed the miracle of the loaves and fishes, transforming five loaves and two fish into enough food for the multitudes in the crowd. It is now evening time, and Jesus sends the crowds away and departs with His disciples.

As you read, keep the following questions in mind: (1) Why does Jesus perform miracles? (2) How would you have responded if you had been in the boat?

> *Immediately Jesus made the disciples get into the boat and go on ahead of him to the other side, while he dismissed the crowd. After he had dismissed them, he went up on a mountainside by himself to pray. When evening came, he was there alone, but the boat was already a considerable distance from land, buffeted by the waves because the wind was against it.*
>
> *During the fourth watch of the night Jesus went out to them, walking on the lake. When the disciples saw him walking on the lake, they were terrified.*
>
> *"It's a ghost," they said, and cried out in fear.*
>
> *But Jesus immediately said to them: "Take courage! It is I. Don't be afraid."*
>
> *"Lord, if it's you," Peter replied, "tell me to come to you on the water."*
>
> *"Come," he said. Then Peter got down out of the boat, walked on the water and came toward Jesus. But when he saw the wind, he was afraid and, beginning to sink, cried out, "Lord, save me!"*
>
> *Immediately Jesus reached out his hand and caught him. "You of little faith," he said, "why did you doubt?"*
>
> *And when they climbed into the boat, the wind died down. Then those who were in the boat worshiped him, saying, "Truly you are the Son of God"* (Matthew 14:22-33).

dig

1. In spite of the busyness of His day, what does Jesus make time to do (see v. 23)?

_____

_____

_____

_____

_____

2. What does this passage say about Peter's faith?

_____

_____

_____

_____

_____

3. What does it mean to "step out in faith"?

_____

_____

_____

_____

_____

_____

4. If you had been Peter and Jesus had invited you to step out in
    faith from the boat to the water, what would you have done?

    _____

    _____

    _____

    _____

    _____

5. Why do you think Jesus performed miracles?

    _____

    _____

    _____

    _____

    _____

6. Often times, the miracles Jesus performed had an impact on
    both the individual to whom they were directed as well as on
    those who saw or heard what had happened. What was the
    direct result of this miracle?

    _____

    _____

    _____

    _____

    _____

apply

1. Write down your own definition of "faith."

    _____

    _____

    _____

    _____

2. In this story, Peter demonstrated his faith in Jesus by stepping
    out onto the water and walking toward Jesus. When have you
    had to step out in faith in your life?

    _____

    _____

    _____

    _____

3. Peter had trusted in Jesus and was upheld. But then, the Bible
    says that Peter saw the wind and became afraid. He began to
    sink, and cried out, "Lord, save me!" (v. 30). What had changed?

    _____

    _____

    _____

    _____

    _____

4. Seconds before, Peter had been walking on the water with Jesus. Now he found himself sinking. Had Jesus stopped holding up Peter?

    _____

    _____

    _____

    _____

5. When it comes to stepping out, do you struggle with doubts? Become fearful? Have a go-for-it attitude? Tentatively do it? Gripe about it? Wait for someone else and then follow him or her? Describe how you handle this call to obedience.

    _____

    _____

    _____

    _____

6. Think of an area of your life in which Jesus is calling you out onto the water. Maybe it is something you feel Him calling you to get involved with or someone whom you sense you are supposed to reach out to. What is holding you back from taking that step of faith and walking toward Jesus?

7. Sometimes it can be hard to know if you should really step out in faith. God's voice is not described as a megaphone announcement or a blaring signal, but as "a still small voice" (1 Kings 19:12, *KJV*). So, how do you know if you are truly hearing God's call?

_____

_____

_____

_____

Here's a checklist for knowing if you should step out in faith on a particular action:

☐ Will it glorify God? In 1 Corinthians 10:31, Paul writes, "Whatever you do, do it for the glory of God."

☐ Is it biblical? Is the action you are considering consistent with God's teachings? In John 14:23, Jesus states, "If anyone loves me, he will obey my teachings."

☐ Do the significant people in my life support it? Oftentimes God uses important people in our lives to help us understand His will.

☐ Do I sense God's leading? Are you sensing a nudge, an urging, an instruction from God to move forward in faith?

8. What do the following verses reveal about faith?

Ephesians 2:8: _____

_____

_____

Mark 10:13-15: _____

_____

_____

Colossians 2:6-7: _____

_____

_____

James 1:5-8: _____

_____

_____

Ephesians 3:16-18: _____

_____

_____

reflect

1. On a scale of 1 to 10, how would you rank your faith in Jesus?

0	1	2	3	4	5	6	7	8	9	10

Limited   Strong

2. How can you work to strengthen your faith?

_____

_____

_____

_____

3. In Mark 10:15, Jesus says that "anyone who will not receive the kingdom of God like a little child will never enter it." Why do you think it is often easier for children than adolescents or adults to have faith?

_____

_____

_____

_____

_____

4. Respond to the following statement: *Doubt is a feeling, but faith is a choice.*

_____

_____

_____

_____

_____

5. Can you still be a Christian and have doubts?

_____

_____

_____

_____

_____

6. Have you ever had doubts in your faith? How did you react
    or respond?

    _____

    _____

    _____

    _____

    _____

Everyone has doubts—it is a natural part of our spiritual life. Here
is a list of suggestions on how to handle doubts:

- **Don't panic when doubt arrives.** Expect it to arrive from
  time to time and be prepared to deal with it.

- **Be honest about your doubts.** Don't be ashamed. Even
  Peter, one of Jesus' closest disciples, had doubts.

- **Don't ignore your doubt.** Ask God and fellow believers to
  help you work it out.

- **Stay in fellowship with others.** Don't drop out. Remember
  that God can use the people in your life to reveal His truth.

- **Seek God.** Through reading the Bible, prayer and worship,
  we allow time for God to speak to us.

- **Be open.** Don't be afraid to think new thoughts and test
  new avenues of faith.

- **Confess.** Continued, unconfessed sin can bring doubt into
  our lives. Ask God to forgive sins that are troubling you.

meditation

Now faith is being sure of what we hope for
and certain of what we do not see.

HEBREWS 11:1

spiritual growth

I don't pig out. I basically eat everything I want;
I've just changed what it is I want to eat.

OPRAH WINFREY

Eat right and exercise. It's the time-tested, simple prescription for good health. We all know that eating right and exercising regularly will promote health, but how many of us really practice what we already know to be true? That's where Oprah can help us out. Listen to her words again: "I basically eat everything I want; I've just changed what it is I want to eat."

Attitude. It makes a big difference in dieting and physical fitness. And a good attitude makes a tremendous difference in spiritual growth. Just like no one can make you healthy, no one can make you grow in your relationship with God. Spiritual growth is an intentional process to develop your friendship with Jesus Christ. A balanced diet of digesting God's Word and exercising your faith in everyday life will help you grow as a Christian.

There are all sorts of temptations to divert your attention away from God. But when you change your desires to God's desires, you'll be able to grow strong in your walk with Christ. The Bible says not to indulge your flesh nature but to hunger for the things of God. Growth in Christ comes from planting and cultivating the fruit of

God's Spirit. By feeding on God's Word, you'll have all the strength you need to put it into practice.

This lesson offers practical tools to help students understand spiritual growth. As you grow in your relationship with God this week, ask God to give you a deep desire and hunger for His Word. The young people you minister to will give you plenty of opportunities to exercise your faith in Christ.

spiritual growth

starter

CHOSEN VOICE: Divide the group into pairs. Give each pair one minute to respond to a random question (such as a favorite childhood memory or the most embarrassing moment). Each partner should talk uninterrupted for the time allotted so that the other can have a chance to get to know his or her partner's voice. Then blindfold one person in each pair and move him or her to one side of the room. Randomly arrange the remaining partners on the other side. Without using their partner's name, they must attempt to get their partner to find them in the room using only their voice. Play until all pairs have been matched. Now watch the introduction to session 8 on *The Christian Life* DVD.

message

Imagine you have some seeds. You plant one in the ground. You wait.

Nothing happens.

So you water it, and soon you notice it begins to grow, pushing its green shoots out from underneath the soil. *It's growing,* you think.

But watering the seed is not enough. In order to have a healthy plant, you must feed, tend, prune and care for the plant. Not just once, either, but continuously throughout the plant's life.

117

Christian faith works much the same way. When you accept Jesus into your life, the seed is planted. But in order to flourish and grow, you must nurture your faith into a blossoming relationship with Jesus Christ.

How is the garden of your faith? Flourishing or lifeless?

In the passage you are about to read from Colossians, Paul is writing to the people of Colosse to encourage them in their spiritual growth. Many of them were being distracted by a growing number of counterfeit religions that were arising in the region. Just as the Starter activity demonstrated, it is easy to get distracted by other voices in our lives. But as we move closer to God, His voice becomes easier to hear (see John 10:27-28).

Paul writes to the Colossians to remind them of their foundation in Jesus and to encourage them to deepen their faith. He says, "So then, just as you received Christ Jesus as Lord, continue to live in him, rooted and built up in him, strengthened in the faith as you were taught and overflowing with thankfulness" (Colossians 2:6-7).

As you read, keep the following questions in mind: (1) What does it mean to grow spiritually? (2) What does it look like in a Christian life? (3) What directions do these verses provide for our spiritual development?

Since, then, you have been raised with Christ, set your hearts on things above, where Christ is seated at the right hand of God. Set your minds on things above, not on earthly things. For you died, and your life is now hidden with Christ in God. When Christ, who is your life, appears, then you also will appear with him in glory.

Put to death, therefore, whatever belongs to your earthly nature: sexual immorality, impurity, lust, evil desires and greed, which is idolatry. Because of these, the wrath of God is coming. You used to walk in these ways, in the life you once lived. But now you must rid yourselves of all such things as these: anger, rage, malice, slander, and filthy language from your lips. Do not lie to each other, since you have taken off your old self with its practices and have put on the new self, which is being renewed in knowledge in the image of its Creator. Here there is no Greek or Jew, circumcised or uncircumcised, barbarian, Scythian, slave or free, but Christ is all, and is in all.

Therefore, as God's chosen people, holy and dearly loved, clothe yourselves with compassion, kindness, humility, gentleness and patience. Bear with each other and forgive whatever grievances you may have against one another. Forgive as the Lord forgave you. And over all these virtues put on love, which binds them all together in perfect unity.

Let the peace of Christ rule in your hearts, since as members of one body you were called to peace. And be thankful. Let the word of Christ dwell in you richly as you teach and admonish one another with all wisdom, and as you sing psalms, hymns and spiritual songs with gratitude in your hearts to God. And whatever you do, whether in word or deed, do it all in the name of the Lord Jesus, giving thanks to God the Father through him (Colossians 3:1-17).

dig

1. Colossians 3:2 says that because you have been raised with Christ, you should set your heart and mind on "things above, not earthly things." What are "things above"?

_____

_____

_____

_____

_____

2. What are "earthly things"?

_____

_____

_____

_____

3. This passage lists a number of attributes associated with our "old self" or "earthly nature" that we should put to death. List as many of them as you can find.

4. Colossians 3:12-17 lists several qualities of our "new selves" in Christ. What are some of the qualities or actions that are characteristic of this new life?

5. Colossians 3:17 states, "Whatever you do, whether in word or in deed, do it all in the name of the Lord Jesus, giving thanks to God the Father through him." What does it mean to "do it all in the name of the Lord Jesus"?

_____

_____

_____

_____

apply

1. What is spiritual growth? How would someone know if he or she were growing?

_____

_____

_____

_____

_____

2. Look back at the list of traits of the old self and new self. Which of these traits do you need to improve?

A trait of my old self I need to work on getting rid of is . . .

_____

_____

_____

A trait of my life in Christ I would like to get better at is . . .

_____

_____

_____

3. For each of the two qualities above, what *specific* actions can you take to become more Christlike in these areas?

_____

_____

_____

_____

_____

4. What do you find the most helpful in growing your faith in the Lord?

_____

_____

_____

_____

_____

5. Read the following verses:

Therefore, rid yourselves of all malice and all deceit, hypocrisy, envy, and slander of every kind. Like newborn babies, crave pure spiritual milk, so that by it you may grow up in your salvation, now that you have tasted that the Lord is good (1 Peter 2:1-3, emphasis added).

We have much to say about this, but it is hard to explain because you are slow to learn. In fact, though by this time you ought to be teachers, you need someone to teach you the elementary truths of God's word all over again. You need milk, *not solid food! Anyone who lives on* milk, *being still an infant, is not acquainted with the teaching about righteousness. But solid food is for the mature, who by constant use have trained themselves to distinguish good from evil* (Hebrews 5:11-14, emphasis added).

What does "milk" symbolize in these passages? Is it something to be desired?

_____

_____

_____

_____

6. Is your Christian walk sustained by milk or solid food?

_____

_____

_____

_____

7. What promise about your spiritual growth can be found in Philippians 1:6?

_____

_____

_____

reflect

1. What is the difference between salvation and spiritual growth?

_____

_____

_____

_____

_____

2. If someone says he or she is feeling spiritually far from God, what advice would you give to that person?

_____

_____

_____

_____

_____

_____

3. How has your faith grown or changed over time?

_____

_____

_____

_____

_____

_____

4. When do you feel closest to God?

_____

_____

_____

_____

_____

5. Do you feel that you are growing spiritually or do you feel stagnant? What actions are you taking in order to nurture your faith?

_____

_____

_____

_____

_____

_____

6. Who has been a major spiritual influence in your life? What is the value of having spiritual role models?

_____

_____

_____

_____

_____

7. Memorizing God's Word so that you can call upon it in times of need is one way to deepen your faith. Do you have a favorite verse or Bible story? If yes, what is it?

_____

_____

_____

_____

_____

meditation

"Then you will call upon me and come and pray to me, and I will listen to you. You will seek me and find me when you seek me with all your heart. I will be found by you," declares the LORD.

JEREMIAH 29:12-14

unit III
God's will

One of my (Jim's) modern-day heroes is Terry Foxe. Terry was a Canadian runner who attempted to run the entire distance from the east coast of Canada to Vancouver, British Columbia, in order to raise money for cancer research. Terry knew the needs of cancer victims intimately because he was one himself—he was running across Canada with an artificial leg. Terry ran 26 miles every day, six days a week, to raise money for cancer.

Terry's enthusiasm and zeal for life caught my attention during his run, and I remember, day after day, seeing him on the news. People, mainly children, would gather around him, and he would usually be standing in front of a microphone in a park or shopping center or church building. He would often say, "I don't know about tomorrow, but I'm thankful for today, and I'm going to make the most of this one day God has given me. I'm going to live one day at a time." I'm not even sure Terry knew that he was quoting Jesus.

Jesus summed up doing the will of God in two simple verses in Matthew 6:33-34: "But seek first his kingdom and his righteousness, and all these things will be given to you as well. Therefore do not worry about tomorrow, for tomorrow will worry about itself: Each day has enough trouble of its own."

In this section, you will have the privilege of helping your students to better understand God's will for their lives and how He reveals that plan through Jesus, the Holy Spirit and the Church. Two of the most often asked questions I receive from kids are "How do I know the will of God?" and "How can I be absolutely sure she/he is the one for me?" Actually, I think we've been asking the wrong questions. Understanding the will of God is probably closer to the Scripture above: (1) seek Him first, and (2) then follow Him one day at a time.

Thanks again for your involvement in kids' lives. The following poem was written by another twentieth-century hero of mine named Sam Shoemaker. He pretty much sums up your important job of working with kids:

I stand by the door.
I neither go too far in, nor stay out.
The door is the most important in the world—
It is the door through which men walk when they find God.
There's no use my going way inside, and staying there,
When so many are still outside and they, as much as I,
Crave to know where the door is.
And all that so many ever find,
Is only the wall where the door ought to be.
They creep along the wall like blind men,
With outstretched, groping hands.
Feeling for a door, knowing there must be a door,
Yet never find it . . .
So I stand by the door.
The most tremendous thing in the world,
Is for men to find that door—the door of God.

the will of God

God will not suffer man to have a knowledge of things to come;
for if he had prescience of his prosperity, he would be careless; and if
understanding of his adversity, he would be despairing and senseless.

AUGUSTINE OF HIPPO

Young people, like many adults, spend a lot of time wondering about God's will for their decisions, future, relationships and circumstances. *What does God think? Does He have all the control, or do I have the power to make my own decisions? How can I know His plan for my life?* This lesson will help students know that God's will can be known and practiced in a way that will make powerful changes in their lives.

When searching for the will of God, it is important not to overlook God Himself. People can spend their lives seeking to discover God's will for each and every situation but miss the wonderful opportunity to know their Creator! God created you to have fellowship with Him (see John 17:3). He gave you His Word as a foundation and guide for your life. Just like a map won't decide for you whether to take the freeway or the highway, God's Word is designed to help you make wise decisions as you journey through life. It was written to help you know and experience a meaningful relationship with God through Jesus Christ. God's Holy Spirit will lead, guide, nudge, protect and provide you with the wisdom to make decisions to honor God (see John 14:26; 16:13-15).

As you prepare for this lesson, spend some time reflecting on God's will for your life. How much time do you spend wondering what God's will is? Do you seek to live out what you already know of His will as given in His Word? How can we focus on knowing God personally instead of constantly looking for specific answers to questions? Knowing God's will for our lives overflows from first knowing God Himself.

the will of God

starter

CHARADE-A-THON: Select four volunteers (A-D) and match them up in pairs (A-B, C-D). Have volunteers A and C go outside the room. As a group, select an activity that could be performed in the room (such as turning on the radio, putting something in the trash, or taking a bite of a piece of food). The task of volunteers B and D will be to each get his or her pair to perform the task without using any words or without directly showing his or her partner what to do. All other creative methods are allowed. Invite volunteers A and C back into the room and begin. Following the charade-a-thon, watch the introduction to session 9 on *The Christian Life* DVD.

message

What is the meaning of life? What is the purpose of our existence? The Bible says that we were created to bring God glory. One of the ways we can bring God praise is by obeying His will.

But what is God's will? How do we discover it? Is it the same for everyone?

As you read the following passage, keep these questions in mind: (1) What do these verses say about God's will for the world? (2) How do we determine God's will?

Praise be to the God and Father of our Lord Jesus Christ, who has blessed us in the heavenly realms with every spiritual blessing in Christ. For he chose us in him before the creation of the world to be holy and blameless in his sight.

In love he predestined us to be adopted as his sons through Jesus Christ, in accordance with his pleasure and will—to the praise of his glorious grace, which he has freely given us in the One he loves. In him we have redemption through his blood, the forgiveness of sins, in accordance with the riches of God's grace that he lavished on us with all wisdom and understanding.

And he made known to us the mystery of his will according to his good pleasure, which he purposed in Christ, to be put into effect when the times will have reached their fulfillment—to bring all things in heaven and on earth together under one head, even Christ.

In him we were also chosen, having been predestined according to the plan of him who works out everything in conformity with the purpose of his will, in order that we, who were the first to hope in Christ, might be for the praise of his glory. And you also were included in Christ when you heard the word of truth, the gospel of your salvation.

Having believed, you were marked in him with a seal, the promised Holy Spirit, who is a deposit guaranteeing our inheritance until the redemption of those who are God's possession—to the praise of his glory (Ephesians 1:3-14).

dig

1. What did Jesus choose for us before we were born?

2. What does "predestination" mean? And what does it mean to be predestined?

3. What was the reason we were predestined to be God's adopted sons and daughters?

4. Reread verses 9-10. What do these verses mean to you?

_____

_____

_____

_____

5. What is the seal that Paul says we have been marked with?

_____

_____

_____

_____

6. Based on these verses, what is God's will for our lives? What is our purpose?

_____

_____

_____

_____

_____

apply

Wouldn't life be easier if we could call God and always get direct and immediate answers to our deepest questions? "Should I go to that party Friday night?" "What college should I go to?" "Is the person I'm dating the right one for me?"

What questions would you ask God about your life? What questions would you ask Him about your future?

_____

_____

_____

_____

_____

_____

Unfortunately, it isn't always as easy as a phone call to discern God's plan for our lives, but He does give us some important tools to use as we strive to discover His will.

the Bible

God's Word can reveal His will for us. "Thy word is a lamp unto my feet, and a light unto my path" (Psalm 119:105, *KJV*). The Bible is our authority when it comes to knowing God's will. Second Timothy 3:16 says, "All Scripture is God-breathed and is useful for teaching, rebuking, correcting and training in righteousness."

As we read and study the Bible, we can know how God wants us to act in many situations. Look up the following verses. What guidelines do they give about how we should live?

2 Timothy 2:23-24: _____

_____

Matthew 6:33-34: _____

_____

Exodus 20:17: _____

_____

James 1:19-20,26: _____

_____

1 Thessalonians 4:3-5: _____

_____

Philippians 4:6: _____

_____

Colossians 3:23-24: _____

_____

Matthew 22:37-39: _____

_____

1 Thessalonians 5:18: _____

_____

The Bible contains a great amount of wisdom on how you should think and act. If you are struggling in a particular area, you can often look in the subject guide or concordance at the back of a Bible to find a list of key words that will help you locate Scriptures on that topic (such as money, pride, worry, fear, and so forth).

However, the Bible will not provide clear guidance for *every* situation you will encounter in life. Nowhere in the Bible will you find an answer as to what college to attend, who you should date, or what career path you should pursue. You likely will find Scriptures that will help you make your decision by providing guidance about godly values, priorities or goals, but nowhere in the Bible will you find the verse, "go to Harvard" or "date Sheila."

When Scripture appears to be silent on a subject, you can look at other indicators to find out the will of God for your life, including turning to the counsel of others, petitioning through prayer, and examining your circumstances.

counsel

God can often use those around you to reveal His will. Proverbs tells us, "Make plans by seeking advice" (20:18) and "where there is no guidance, the people fall; but in abundance of counselors there is victory" (11:14, *NASB*).

To whom can you go for good, solid, sound advice? What makes him or her a worthy advisor?

_____

_____

_____

_____

You need people in your life to whom you can go for Christian advice and counsel. Oftentimes, God can use these individuals to help you discover His will. But while God is perfect and infallible, people are human and prone to making mistakes and exercising poor judgment. So consider these people's advice, but weigh their thoughts alongside relevant Scriptures and personal prayer.

prayer

Earlier in session 7, we talked about the "still, small voice" of God. Prayer is one way of hearing God's voice. People often assume that prayer is just about talking to God, but some of the most powerful moments in your prayer life may come when you take the time to listen.

It's not always easy to be quiet and still. The world moves at a frantic pace, and often we expect God to do the same. Life might seem so much easier if God could just text us His will or email it so that we could read it when we had the time. But try it this week. Set aside some time to just listen to God. James tells us to ask God for wisdom, expecting Him to give it to us generously (see James 1:5-8), but we must be receptive and available to hearing it.

1. Read Philippians 4:6-7. What does Paul suggest you do instead of worrying about God's will?

    _____

    _____

    _____

2. What things do you need to stop worrying about and present to God in prayer?

    _____

    _____

    _____

3. Read James 4:7-8. How does submitting yourself to God and resisting the devil help you draw near and listen to God?

    _____

    _____

    _____

circumstances

At times, you can also come to know the will of God through your circumstances. Proverbs 16:9 tells us, "In his heart a man plans his course, but the Lord determines his steps." Perhaps you have heard someone say that a "door closed" on one opportunity but opened to provide another option.

1. Describe a time when your circumstances seemed to lead you down a particular path by opening or closing a particular door.

2. Read Proverbs 3:5-6. There are three directives given in these verses, but each has the same result. What are these?

If we . . .   then God will . . .

Be sure not to act impulsively based solely on your circumstances. Seek the will of God through the other methods of prayer, Scripture reading and the wise counsel of others to help you determine if the circumstances are from God.

reflect

1. Describe a time in your life when you clearly sensed God's will.
    How did you discern it?

    _____

    _____

    _____

    _____

    _____

2. Are there any issues in your life you need or want to give over
    to the will of God? List them.

    _____

    _____

    _____

    _____

    _____

3. What is hard about submitting to the will of God? What is
    easy about it?

    _____

    _____

    _____

    _____

4. Which is more difficult for you to do: discern God's will, obey God's will, or trust God's plan for your life?

_____

_____

_____

_____

_____

5. Sometimes you will make a wrong decision. How does that fit into God's will?

_____

_____

_____

_____

_____

_____

6. Do you think there is ever more than one option that would fit into God's will?

_____

_____

_____

_____

_____

7. Read Romans 12:1-2. What do these verses say you have to do
    to be able to discern God's will?

    _____

    _____

    _____

    _____

    _____

8. First Thessalonians 5:18 says that we are to "give thanks in all
    circumstances." Notice that this verse says *in* all circum-
    stances, not *for* all circumstances. What is the difference be-
    tween the two? How can you learn to give thanks in the midst
    of your circumstances?

    _____

    _____

    _____

    _____

    _____

9. Does God have the perfect college choice, career or person to
    marry picked out for you?

    _____

    _____

    _____

    _____

meditation

Do not conform any longer to the pattern of this world,
but be transformed by the renewing of your mind. Then
you will be able to test and approve what God's will is—
his good, pleasing and perfect will.

ROMANS 12:2

Jesus

The most pressing question on the problem of faith is whether a man as a civilized being can believe in the divinity of the Son of God, Jesus Christ, for therein rests the whole of our faith.

FYODOR DOSTOEVSKY

"Who do you say that I am?" Jesus' question to Peter causes both believers and nonbelievers alike to really consider who Jesus claimed to be. Although certain New Testament scholars have given themselves the task of trying to deconstruct the life of Christ, Peter's response to Jesus offers everyone the hope of a transforming relationship with God. Jesus is the Messiah sent to save the world.

Helping young people develop a deeper walk with Jesus Christ affirms God's work in your life. By serving teenagers for the Kingdom, you are declaring to Jesus, "You are the Christ, the Son of the living God." Helping someone to discover a personal friendship with Jesus is the best gift you could ever give. It's also a gift that you never want to ignore or neglect.

Before you rush out to prepare this lesson, spend some time with Jesus. Think about His presence in your life. How would you describe your relationship with Him right now? What struggles or frustrations do you need to give Him today?

Jesus Christ, the Son of the living God, wants you to know Him more and more. Every day is a new chance to be freed of yesterday's regrets. Every day is an opportunity for you to rest in His unconditional love. Although some people want to strip Jesus down to nothing, He wants to build into you how very essential He is to your life.

group study guide

Jesus

starter

WHO AM I? Write the names of several well-known people (such as celebrities, icons, historical figures or fictional characters) on pieces of tape and have each group member put one on their forehead or back. Each member must try to guess who they are by asking other group members yes or no questions until everyone has discovered their identity. Next, watch the introduction to session 10 on *The Christian Life* DVD.

message

How would your friends describe you? Your family? Your teachers? Your enemies? How would they respond if you asked them, "Who do you say I am?" Would you want to know the answer?

This is just what Jesus did with His disciple Peter.

In the following verses from Matthew, Jesus is traveling with Peter and the other disciples through a territory called Caesarea

Philippi—an area that was hostile to the Christian faith. It is here that Jesus asks Peter two questions: (1) "Who do the people say [I] am?" and (2) "Who do you say I am?"

Read on to find out Peter's response. As you read, keep the following questions in mind: (1) Does Peter really understand who Jesus is? (2) If a friend asked you to describe Jesus, who would *you* say He is?

> *When Jesus came to the region of Caesarea Philippi, he asked his disciples, "Who do people say the Son of Man is?"*
>
> *They replied, "Some say John the Baptist; others say Elijah; and still others, Jeremiah or one of the prophets."*
>
> *"But what about you?" he asked. "Who do you say I am?"*
>
> *Simon Peter answered, "You are the Christ, the Son of the living God."*
>
> *Jesus replied, "Blessed are you, Simon son of Jonah, for this was not revealed to you by man, but by my Father in heaven."*
>
> *Then he warned his disciples not to tell anyone that he was the Christ* (Matthew 16:13-17,20).

dig

1. Why do you think Jesus asked Peter what people were saying about Him?

   _____

   _____

   _____

   _____

   _____

2. According to Peter's response, who were some of the individuals that people believed Jesus was?

_____

_____

_____

_____

3. Who does Peter say that Jesus is?

_____

_____

_____

_____

4. According to the text, how did Peter understand who Jesus is?

_____

_____

_____

_____

5. Why did Jesus not want them to tell anyone He was Christ?

_____

_____

_____

_____

apply

Light of the World. King. Creator. High Priest. Holy One. Rabbi.
Lamb of God. Redeemer. The Way. The Truth. The True Vine. The
Righteous One. Savior. There are many names associated with Jesus. But who did Jesus say that He was? Let's take a look at the ac-
tual words Jesus used to describe Himself and see how we can better
understand who He is based on what He claimed about Himself.

1. Read the following verses and determine who Jesus says He is
    in each verse.

    John 14:6: _____

    _____

    John 10:29-30: _____

    _____

    Revelation 1:8: _____

    _____

    John 5:22,27: _____

    _____

    John 3:17: _____

    _____

    John 4:25-26: _____

    _____

    John 1:1,14: _____

    _____

2. One of the hardest aspects to understand about Jesus is that He is both fully God and fully man. What do you think "fully God and fully man" really means?

_____

_____

_____

fully man

1. Look up Hebrews 2:17-18 and Hebrews 4:15. What do these verses reveal about Jesus' being fully human?

_____

_____

_____

_____

2. How do these verses provide comfort for you when you face trials and struggles?

_____

_____

_____

_____

3. What aspect of Jesus' human nature are shown in the following verses?

Galatians 4:4-5: _____

_____

Matthew 26:36-42: _____

_____

John 11:30-35: _____

_____

Mark 11:12: _____

_____

Jesus can sympathize with the difficulties we face because He lived on this earth as a human being. He slept. He ate. He experienced joy and sadness. He enjoyed the company of friends and experienced the ache of loneliness. Being fully human means that He can identify with *all* aspects of our lives.

fully God

At the same time, Jesus is fully God. He has the power to heal the sick, forgive sins, mend lives and raise the dead. What can we learn about Jesus' being fully God from the following passages?

John 1:1-4: _____

_____

_____

John 8:23-24: _____

_____

_____

Mark 2:5-7: _____

_____

_____

John 10:25-30: _____

_____

_____

John 14:9-11: _____

_____

_____

reflect

1. Jesus says, "I am the way and the truth and the life" (John 14:6). What things of the world try to compete with Jesus as the way?

_____

_____

_____

_____

_____

2. What would you say to someone who believed that Jesus was just a good man but nothing more?

_____

_____

_____

_____

3. What comfort can you gain by knowing that Jesus was both fully human and fully God?

_____

_____

_____

_____

4. In his book *Mere Christianity*, Christian author and theologian C. S. Lewis makes the following claim:

> A man who was merely a man and said the sort of things Jesus said would not be a great moral teacher. He would either be a lunatic—on the level with a man who says he is a poached egg—or he would be the devil of hell. You must take your choice. Either this was, and is, the Son of God, or else a madman or something worse. You can shut Him up for a fool or you can fall at His feet and call Him Lord and God. But let us not come with any patronizing nonsense about His being a great human teacher. He has not left that open to us."[1]

In essence, Lewis is saying that there are three possibilities for who Jesus was: a liar, a lunatic or truly Lord. If a friend asked you, "Who is Jesus?" how would you respond?

_____

_____

_____

_____

meditation

I am the way and the truth and the life.
No one comes to the Father except through me.

JOHN 14:6

Note

1. C. S. Lewis, *Mere Christianity* (New York: Macmillan Publishing, 1943), p. 56.

the Holy Spirit

*In Michelangelo's famous painting on the ceiling of the Sistine Chapel,
God is reaching out to Adam. Their hands never quite touch. The Holy
Spirit is the missing touch of God.*

JAMES BRYAN SMITH

When the musician Sting sang, "We are spirits in the material world,"
he probably wasn't trying to make any bold theological statement
about our true nature. However, he was right. The core of our being
is spirit and this material world we live in is only a temporary dwell-
ing (see 2 Corinthians 4:16). As individuals designed by God, we
were created to fellowship with Him for all of eternity.

God sent His Son, Jesus Christ, to bring us back into fellowship
with Him. Through the blood of Jesus, our spirit can be reunited in
fellowship with God (see 1 Corinthians 6:17). It's the living presence of Jesus, the Holy Spirit, that helps us to obey and understand
God (see John 16:16-21; 16:13-15). Being empowered by God through
the Spirit, we can do all things through Christ. Without the Spirit
in our lives, we can do nothing. The Spirit is the empowering divine

nature that frees us from the bondage of sin and death (see Romans 8:13). It is on the Holy Spirit that we rely for help, guidance, protection, peace and security in this insecure world.

At times, we forget that the Holy Spirit is as much a member of the Trinity as are the Father and the Son. The Father and the Son get a lot of attention, but the Holy Spirit tends to get left out of the picture. Don't we realize that it is the Holy Spirit who empowers us to walk in the steps of Jesus?

Allow this study to develop a greater love for the Holy Spirit in you. Ask yourself how you can yield your heart, mind and spirit to the work of the Holy Spirit as He leads, guides and protects your every move. God deeply desires for you to walk in His Spirit. He wants the fruit of the Holy Spirit to nourish the young people He has placed in your care. Through the Holy Spirit, you have a reservoir of power in your life like nothing else in this material world.

the Holy Spirit

starter

DRAWING ON FAITH: Divide the group into pairs and give each pair a piece of paper. Ask each pair to spend two minutes discussing who the Holy Spirit is and what is the Holy Spirit's role in our lives. Then give each pair five minutes to represent the Holy Spirit in a drawing. Allow time at the end for each pair to explain and share their illustration. Once you have finished, watch the introduction to session 11 on *The Christian Life* DVD.

message

The following passage from the book of John takes place during the last 24 hours of Jesus' life on Earth. In John 13–17, Jesus attempted to explain to His disciples the significant events that were about to occur. He patiently answered their questions and repeatedly explained points until they began to grasp the magnitude of His proclamations. It is in John 16 that Jesus began to explain to them that even though He would soon be leaving them, He would send the Holy Spirit to comfort and guide them.

But who—or what—is the Holy Spirit? Christians believe that the Holy Spirit is a member of the Trinity and that He dwells within us, providing comfort, guidance, power and assurance. Although the word "trinity" is never directly used in the Bible, the concept of a triune God, or three persons in one—Father, Son and Holy Spirit— is evident throughout the Scriptures (see Matthew 28:19).

As you read this passage in John, keep the following questions in mind: (1) What did Jesus say the Holy Spirit would do in our lives? (2) Have you ever felt the presence of the Holy Spirit in your life, guiding or directing you?

> *Now I am going to him who sent me, yet none of you asks me, "Where are you going?" Because I have said these things, you are filled with grief. But I tell you the truth: It is for your good that I am going away.*
>
> *Unless I go away, the Counselor will not come to you; but if I go, I will send him to you. When he comes, he will convict the world of guilt in regard to sin and righteousness and judgment: in regard to sin, because men do not believe in me; in regard to righteousness, because I am going to the Father, where you can see me no longer; and in regard to judgment, because the prince of this world now stands condemned.*
>
> *I have much more to say to you, more than you can now bear. But when he, the Spirit of truth, comes, he will guide you into all truth. He will not speak on his own; he will speak only what he hears, and he will tell you what is yet to come. He will bring glory to me by taking from what is mine and making it known to you. All that belongs to the Father is mine.*
>
> *That is why I said the Spirit will take from what is mine and make it known to you (John 16:5-15).*

dig

1. What is Jesus referring to when He says that He is "going to him who sent me"?

2. Why does Jesus tell the disciples, "It is for your good that I am going away"?

3. Who does Jesus call the Holy Spirit? What does this tell you about the role the Holy Spirit will play in your life?

4. Why did the Holy Spirit come? List the reasons for the Holy Spirit's coming from Jesus' teaching in this passage.

   Verse 7: _____

   _____

   Verse 8: _____

   _____

   Verse 13: _____

   _____

   Verse 14: _____

   _____

5. According to this passage, is the Holy Spirit a separate entity from God with a mind of His own?

   _____

   _____

   _____

6. In Philippians 4:13, Paul states, "I can do everything through him who gives me strength." In what areas of your life do you need to cling to this promise and rely on the support of the Holy Spirit?

   _____

   _____

   _____

   _____

apply

So what is the purpose of the Holy Spirit? Primarily, the Holy Spirit's purpose is to be with us in the absence of Jesus, but the Bible also reveals four specific roles of the Holy Spirit.

to dwell inside us

1. Read 1 Corinthians 3:16. In this verse, what does it mean to be God's "temple"?

    _____

    _____

    _____

    _____

2. Read 1 Corinthians 6:18-20. From what particular type of sins does this verse say we must flee?

    _____

    _____

    _____

    _____

3. How does Paul state these sins are different?

    _____

    _____

    _____

    _____

4. How are you obeying verse 20, "Therefore honor God with your body"?

_____

_____

_____

to empower us to live the christian life

1. What do these verses state about how the Holy Spirit helps us?

Romans 14:17: _____

_____

_____

1 Corinthians 2:6-12: _____

_____

_____

Romans 8:26-27: _____

_____

_____

Romans 5:5: _____

_____

_____

1 Corinthians 12:4-11: _____

_____

_____

2. In order to have the power of God working in your life, you
    must surrender and submit yourself to the control of the
    Holy Spirit. How can you best surrender and submit yourself
    to God?

    _____

    _____

    _____

    _____

to provide us with the power to witness

Jesus doesn't say that you can share your faith when you want to,
when it's convenient or when you are comfortable with doing so.
He commands each of us in the Great Commission to "go and make
disciples of all nations" (Matthew 28:19). Fortunately, God provides the Holy Spirit to aid in this task.

1. Acts 1:7-8 records Jesus' final words to His disciples. What
    promise did He give to them?

    _____

    _____

    _____

2. What intimidates you the most about sharing the gospel
    with others?

    _____

    _____

    _____

3. Do you find it easier to share your faith with friends or with strangers? Why?

_____

_____

_____

_____

_____

4. Read Mark 13:10-11. How can this verse reassure us as we move forward to share our faith with others?

_____

_____

_____

_____

_____

5. Who are the individuals in your life with whom you could share your faith? List their names here.

_____

_____

_____

_____

_____

to give us the assurance of our salvation

1. According to Ephesians 1:13-14, what does the Holy Spirit do for us?

_____

_____

_____

_____

_____

2. What assurance is found in Romans 8:16-17?

_____

_____

_____

_____

_____

3. According to Romans 8:26-27, what is the benefit of having the Holy Spirit reside within?

_____

_____

_____

_____

_____

reflect

1. What does it mean to "walk in the Spirit" or "live by the Spirit"?

2. What keeps believers from submitting to God's Spirit?

3. Describe a time when you felt the presence of the Holy Spirit in your life guiding or directing you.

4. What is the Holy Spirit doing in your life today, this week, this month?

Do you need a fresh start with the Holy Spirit? To prepare your heart for the guiding and empowering of the Holy Spirit, you must:

1. **Desire to live for God.** "Blessed are those who hunger and thirst for righteousness, for they will be filled" (Matthew 5:6).

2. **Be willing to surrender and submit your will (life) to God.** "Therefore, I urge you, brothers, in view of God's mercy, to offer your bodies as living sacrifices, holy and pleasing to God—this is your spiritual act of worship. Do not conform any longer to the pattern of this world, but be transformed by the renewing of your mind. Then you will be able to test and approve what God's will is—his good, pleasing and perfect will" (Romans 12:1-2).

3. **Confess your sins.** "If we confess our sins, he is faithful and just and will forgive us our sins and purify us from all unrighteousness" (1 John 1:9).

4. **Be filled with the Spirit.** "Do not get drunk on wine, which leads to debauchery. Instead, be filled with the Spirit" (Ephesians 5:18).

5. **Live by the Spirit.** "So I say, live by the Spirit, and you will not gratify the desires of the sinful nature" (Galatians 5:16).

meditation

And I will ask the Father, and he will give you
another Counselor to be with you forever—the Spirit
of truth. The world cannot accept him, because it neither
sees him nor knows him. But you know him, for he lives
with you and will be in you. I will not leave you
as orphans; I will come to you.

JOHN 14:15-18

session 12

the church

Therefore, we are ambassadors for Christ, as though
God were entreating through us.

2 CORINTHIANS 5:20

For every student who confesses Jesus as Lord, each one has a spiritual gift just waiting to be used for God's glory. You have the exciting opportunity to help teenagers use their gifts for God and understand their role in the Body of Christ. When young people discover that they are ambassadors for God, their whole life takes on a new dimension.

Many young people have a negative view of church. To them, church is dull, boring and irrelevant. Perhaps it's because they've always been on the outside looking in. Maybe it's because nobody ever took the time to help them discover their spiritual gifts. Can you imagine what this world would be like if every student in your youth ministry understood their purpose and function in the Body of Christ?

You can help teenagers become missionaries for God by helping them see that God wants to use them to influence their families and friends for His kingdom. This lesson will be a great primer to develop leadership in your youth ministry. The most powerful student ministries are the ones with strong student leadership. Students have the chance to discover that the Church isn't a thing or place but Christ living out His presence in their lives. Today, God wants you to set your students on fire for Christ.

the church

starter

GOING WITHOUT: In this exercise, get the students together as a group to discuss the following questions: If you had to give up one of your abilities, which of the following would be the hardest to let go? Which would be the easiest to let go? Why?

- use of your legs
- use of your arms
- your memory
- your sight
- your speech
- your hearing

Now watch the introduction to session 12 on *The Christian Life* DVD.

message

How do you view "church"? Is it something you look forward to? Something you dread? Do you see yourself as an active participant or as a shadow in the pew? Do you believe that you have a role to play in your body of believers? What if I told you that your church— your youth group—could not be what God intended it to be without you in it . . . that you have something valuable and vital to add to it. Something only *you* can provide. Would you honestly be able to say that you are doing your part?

In the following passage, Paul is writing to the believers in Corinth. Prior to his arrival, Corinth had been a city of loose morals and shady characters. But in a display of God's power to use the lowliest of things to bring glory to Himself, the church in Corinth became one of the largest churches in the area. However, a few years later, Paul received word that the Corinthians had fallen back into some of their old habits. First Corinthians is Paul's letter to try to get them back on track, and these verses in particular examine the importance of each person's role in the Body of Christ.

As you read this passage, keep the following questions in mind: (1) What does the "body" represent in this passage? (2) What happens if one of the parts of the body doesn't do its job?

The body is a unit, though it is made up of many parts; and though all its parts are many, they form one body. So it is with Christ. For we were all baptized by one Spirit into one body—whether Jews or Greeks, slave or free—and we were all given the one Spirit to drink.

Now the body is not made up of one part but of many. If the foot should say, "Because I am not a hand, I do not belong to the body," it would not for that reason cease to be part of the body. And if the ear should say, "Because I am not an eye, I do not belong to the body," it would not for that reason cease to be part of the body. If the whole body were an eye, where would the sense of hearing be? If the whole body were an ear, where would the sense of smell be? But in fact God has arranged the parts in the body, every one of them, just as he wanted them to be. If they were all one part, where would the body be? As it is, there are many parts, but one body.

The eye cannot say to the hand, "I don't need you!" And the head cannot say to the feet, "I don't need you!" On the contrary, those parts of the body that seem to be weaker are indispensable, and the parts that we think are less honorable we treat with special honor. And the parts that are unpresentable are treated with special modesty, while our presentable parts need no special treatment. But God has combined the members of the body and has given greater honor to the parts that lacked it, so that there should be no division in the body, but that its parts should have equal concern for each other. If one part suffers, every part suffers with it; if one part is honored, every part rejoices with it.

Now you are the body of Christ, and each one of you is a part of it. And in the church God has appointed first of all apostles, second prophets, third teachers, then workers of miracles, also those having gifts of healing, those able to help others, those with gifts of administration, and those speaking in different kinds of tongues. Are all apostles? Are all prophets? Are all teachers? Do all work miracles? Do all have gifts of healing? Do all speak in tongues? Do all interpret? But eagerly desire the greater gifts (1 Corinthians 12:12-31).

dig

1. Why is the Church called "the body of Christ"?

_____

_____

_____

2. In the analogy in the passage, what happens to a part if it decides it doesn't want to be a member of the body anymore? What are the consequences for the body as a whole?

3. How are the parts related to each other?

4. What comfort can we gain from the fact that God "has arranged the parts in the body, every one of them, just as he wanted them to be" (v. 18)?

5. What does Paul say about the importance and treatment of various body parts (see vv. 22-24)? How does this relate to the Church?

_____

_____

_____

_____

_____

6. How is the body strengthened by being made up of different parts?

_____

_____

_____

_____

_____

apply

1. Think about your church. List all the roles—paid or volunteer—that people play at your church.

_____

_____

_____

_____

2. There are a number of passages in the Bible that discuss spiritual gifts. Look up the following and create a partial list of some of the spiritual gifts mentioned in these passages.

1 Corinthians 12:28-30   Romans 12:4-8   1 Corinthians 12:4-10

3. Think about your own gifts and talents—things that you are naturally good at or naturally drawn to. What spiritual gifts do you believe you have? (Note: Sometimes it can be difficult to ascribe spiritual gifts to yourself. If you and your group feel comfortable, ask others to suggest the spiritual gifts they see exhibited in you.)

4. It can be tempting to view this passage as just a feel-good, everyone-is-special passage. But it is more than that. Not only is Paul stating that every role in the Body of Christ is of value, but he is also saying that every role is essential. There is no room for passivity. The eye must see; the ear must hear. Now read Matthew 25:14-30. Who does the master reward in this story? Why?

5. Explain the analogy between the servants and the talents and us and our spiritual gifts. What is the lesson?

6. Are you actively fulfilling your role in the youth group? In your church? In the Body of Christ? In what ways?

reflect

1. Describe your views of church. Is it something you enjoy? Something you value?

   _____

   _____

   _____

   _____

   _____

   _____

2. What is the purpose of church?

   _____

   _____

   _____

   _____

   _____

3. How do people discover what spirituals gifts they have?

   _____

   _____

   _____

   _____

   _____

   _____

4. If you see yourself as a passive member of the Body, what is keeping you from getting involved?

_____

_____

_____

_____

_____

5. Based on this Scripture passage in 1 Corinthians, what is the result—for you personally and for the Church as a whole—if you just sit on the sidelines and not participate?

_____

_____

_____

_____

_____

6. Where or in what ways do you feel called to be involved as an active member of the Body of Christ?

_____

_____

_____

_____

_____

meditation

Just as each of us has one body with many members,

and these members do not all have the same function,

so in Christ we who are many form one body,

and each member belongs to all the others.

ROMANS 12:4-5

HOMEWORD

WHERE PARENTS GET REAL ANSWERS

Get Equipped with HomeWord...

LISTEN
HomeWord Radio
programs reach over 800 communities nationwide with *HomeWord with Jim Burns* – a daily ½ hour interview feature, *HomeWord Snapshots* – a daily 1 minute family drama, and *HomeWord this Week* – a ½ hour weekend edition of the daily program, and our one-hour program.

CLICK
HomeWord.com
provides advice and resources to millions of visitors each year. A truly interactive website, HomeWord.com provides access to parent newsletter, Q&As, online broadcasts, tip sheets, our online store and more.

READ
HomeWord Resources
parent newsletters, equip families and Churches worldwide with practical Q&As, online broadcasts, tip sheets, our online store and more. Many of these resources are also packaged digitally to meet the needs of today's busy parents.

ATTEND
HomeWord Events
Understanding Your Teenager, Building Healthy Morals & Values, Generation 2 Generation and Refreshing Your Marriage are held in over 100 communities nationwide each year. HomeWord events educate and encourage parents while providing answers to life's most pressing parenting and family questions.

A Ministry with *Jim Burns*

In response to the overwhelming needs of parents and families, Jim Burns founded HomeWord in 1985. HomeWord, a Christian organization, equips and encourages parents, families, and churches worldwide.

Find Out More
Sign up for our FREE daily e-devotional and parent e-newsletter at HomeWord.com, or call 800.397.9725.

HomeWord.com

Small Group Curriculum Kits

Confident Parenting Kit

This is a must-have resource for today's family! Let Jim Burns help you to tackle overcrowded lives, negative family patterns, while creating a grace-filled home and raising kids who love God and themselves.

Kit contains:
- 6 sessions on DVD featuring Dr. Jim Burns
- CD with reproducible small group leader's guide and participant guides
- poster, bulletin insert, and more

Creating an Intimate Marriage Kit

Dr. Jim Burns wants every couple to experience a marriage filled with A.W.E.: affection, warmth, and encouragement. He shows husbands and wives how to make their marriage a priority as they discover ways to repair the past, communicate and resolve conflict, refresh their marriage spiritually, and more!

Kit contains:
- 6 sessions on DVD featuring Dr. Jim Burns
- CD with reproducible small group leader's guide and participant guides
- poster, bulletin insert, and more

Parenting Teenagers for Positive Results

This popular resource is designed for small groups and Sunday schools. The DVD features real family situations played out in humorous family vignettes followed by words of wisdom by youth and family expert, Jim Burns, Ph.D.

Kit contains:
- 6 sessions on DVD featuring Dr. Jim Burns
- CD with reproducible small group leader's guide and participant guides
- poster, bulletin insert, and more

Teaching Your Children Healthy Sexuality Kit

Trusted family authority Dr. Jim Burns outlines a simple and practical guide for parents on how to develop in their children a healthy perspective regarding their bodies and sexuality. Promotes godly values about sex and relationships.

Kit contains:
- 6 sessions on DVD featuring Dr. Jim Burns
- CD with reproducible small group leader's guide and participant guides
- poster, bulletin insert, and more

Parent and Family Resources from HomeWord for you and your kids...

One Life Kit

Your kids only have one life – help them discover the greatest adventure life has to offer! 50 fresh devotional readings that cover many of the major issues of life and faith your kids are wrestling with such as sex, family relationships, trusting God, worry, fatigue and daily surrender. And it's perfect for you and your kids to do together!

Addicted to God Kit

Is your kids' time absorbed by MySpace, text messaging and hanging out at the mall? This devotional will challenge them to adopt thankfulness, make the most of their days and never settle for mediocrity! Fifty days in the Scripture is bound to change your kids' lives forever.

Devotions on the Run Kit

These devotionals are short, simple, and spiritual. They will encourage you to take action in your walk with God. Each study stays in your heart throughout the day, providing direction and clarity when it is most needed.

90 Days Through the New Testament Kit

Downloadable devotional. Author Jim Burns put together a Bible study devotional program for himself to follow, one that would take him through the New Testament in three months. His simple plan was so powerful that he was called to share it with others. A top seller!

Tons of helpful resources for youth workers, parents and youth. Visit our online store at www.HomeWord.com or call us at 800-397-9725

HOME WORD
WHERE PARENTS GET REAL ANSWERS

Small Group Curriculum Kits

Confirming Your Faith Kit

Rite-of-Passage curriculum empowers youth to make wise decisions...to choose Christ. Help them take ownership of their faith! Lead them to do this by experiencing a vital Christian lifestyle.

Kit contains:
- 13 engaging lessons
- Ideas for retreats and special Celebration
- Solid foundational Bible concepts
- 1 leaders guide and 6 student journals (booklets)

10 Building Blocks Kit

Learn to live, laugh, love, and play together as a family. When you learn the 10 essential principles for creating a happy, close-knit household, you'll discover a family that shines with love for God and one another! Use this curriculum to help equip families in your church.

Kit contains:
- 10 sessions on DVD featuring Dr. Jim Burns
- CD with reproducible small group leader's guide and participant guides
- poster and bulletin insert
- 10 Building Blocks book

How to Talk to Your Kids About Drugs Kit

Dr. Jim Burns speaks to parents about the important topic of talking to their kids about drugs. You'll find everything you need to help parents learn and implement a plan for drug-proofing their kids.

Kit contains:
- 2 session DVD featuring family expert Dr. Jim Burns
- CD with reproducible small group leader's guide and participant guides
- poster, bulletin insert, and more
- How to Talk to Your Kids About Drugs book

everybody's got a gift

spiritual gifts
Jim Burns and *Doug Fields, General Editors*
ISBN 978.08307.46453

The gifts of the Spirit aren't like the right to vote—you don't have to be at least 18 to exercise them. Although it may be hard for some teens to believe, they are all uniquely gifted by God to make a mark for His kingdom . . . starting now! *Spiritual Gifts*, part of the new *Uncommon* youth curriculum series created by veteran youth minister Jim Burns, includes a youth-friendly spiritual gifts inventory tool that will enable your entire group to discover and begin to use their unique combination of gifts. Twelve sessions of youth-friendly Bible study will help the teens in your group come alive with purpose, excitement and Spirit-focused power! Use *Uncommon* youth Bible studies with the *Uncommon* DVD series, which include session intros from Jim Burns and reproducible student handouts for every session.

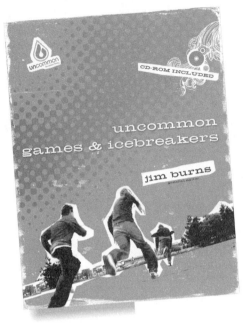